Victory *through* DEFEAT

Lessons through the life of Jospeh

George Mwansa

Victory *through* DEFEAT

Dedicated to my children Mwape and Brainerd Mwila.
May this book inspire you to live in the
heavenly realms with Christ Jesus.

First published in 2010, this edition printed 2016.

British Library Cataloguing in Publication Data. A catalogue
record for this book is available from the British Library.

ISBN: 978-1-78665-005-4

Published by The Stanborough Press, Grantham, Lincolnshire.
Printed in China.
Designed by Abigail Murphy

contents

Victory *through* **DEFEAT**

Introduction

On 6 March 2005, my wife Martha, a wonderful companion of sixteen blessed years, died in a road traffic accident near Serenje, Zambia. In a bid to find meaning out of that tragedy, I turned to the story of Joseph recorded in Genesis chapters 39-46. The book you hold in your hands is the product of that fruitful study. I pray that it will bless your heart and help you to have a deeper relationship with God.

George Mwansa

Chapter 1

The growing-up years

'Joseph, a young man of seventeen, was tending the flocks with his brothers, the sons of Bilhah and the sons of Zilpah, his father's wives, and he brought their father a bad report about them.' (Genesis 37:2.)

Joseph was born and bred in a polygamous family. His father Jacob had two wives, Leah and Rachel, who were actually sisters! Jacob had six sons and a daughter, Dinah, through Leah. Their names were Reuben, Simeon, Levi, Judah, Issachar and Zebulun. Jacob's sons through Rachel were Joseph and Benjamin. Through Leah and Rachel's maidservants, Zilpah and Bilhah, Jacob had Gad, Asher, Dan and Naphtali. All those children were born to him in Paddan Aram. (See Genesis 35:23-26.)

It is with a good reason that the Bible mentions Joseph's age when he enters the pages of sacred history. A lad of seventeen then as today would be considered just that – a lad. What makes Joseph special is his spiritual alertness. Naturally, we would have assumed that Reuben, being the oldest, would have been the most spiritual. However, spirituality and age are not synonymous. Writing to young Timothy, Paul says: 'Don't let anyone look down on you because you are young, but set an example for the believers in speech, in life, in love, in faith and in purity.' (1 Timothy 4:12.) At the age of seventeen Joseph was already connected to the source of life – God.

Many young people nowadays think that spirituality is something they can assign to the future. At seventeen, life is just beginning; why waste it on serious reflection? After all, they still have a long life ahead. But in reasoning this way they blunder and often at their peril. There is no better time for them to connect with God than early

Victory *through* **DEFEAT**

in life. There are many advantages and no disadvantages in doing this. The early stage affords them an opportunity to build a good and solid Christian foundation. Starting the important journey of life requires knowledge of the basic ins and outs. No one can offer that opportunity better than God, the Author of life. Unfortunately for many young people, television, the Internet and a host of other mass-media outlets are the building blocks of that critical foundation. Building this early foundation with God helps to protect them from the foolish and often tragic mistakes many young people make.

Jeffrey grew up in a nice home where comfort and her twin sister ease kept him company. His parents who hailed from humble backgrounds made sure that they provided for their children adequately, affording them the comfort they, themselves, had been denied when they were young. Though Jeffrey's parents went to church regularly, religion was not a major factor in the home. At that critical time when the foundation is laid, Jeffrey learnt to smoke pot, drink alcohol and had an insatiable appetite for watching television. Suffice it to say that Jeffrey's life, ruined early, became only a burden to himself and his parents. The demons of alcohol and drugs haunted him constantly throughout his adult life.

By the time she was sixteen, Jane had securely built for herself a foundation where sex was the cornerstone. Advice about the dangers of such a reckless lifestyle fell on deaf ears. Jane would often say: 'All of us will die, some from AIDS, others from accidents and still others from other causes.' One day trouble began to rain on her life. She was shattered as she saw her sandy foundation collapse. Disease after disease and a number of failed marriages became her sad lot.

The one safe decision we must make early in life is to connect with God. With God, life becomes so much sweeter, so much more

1   *The growing-up years*

peaceful and so much more secure!

Jesus, our perfect example, grew that way. Right from birth his was a life hidden in God. Jesus came to our world out of Mary's womb and lived every step in the presence of his Father as he pursued his mission of saving humanity.

Often I bump into Christian young people who don't even think about baptism. The question I usually ask them is whether they love the Lord or not. Every single one of them answers in the affirmative. I then ask: 'Are you baptised?' A good number will say they are not. Most of them reason that they are still young. 'I know that it is important to be baptised,' one of them said, 'but I am still young. I could easily fall into sin and get disfellowshipped. I shall be baptised when I grow old. That way I won't fall into sin.' They forget that every good decision one makes today makes it easier the next time to make another good one. When we put off an important decision, we are simply making it doubly hard to make that same decision at a future date. What we intend to become tomorrow we must begin to become today. For this reason the Bible says: 'Today, if you hear his voice, do not harden your hearts.' (Hebrews 4:7.) When the heart is hardened today it will not be easy to soften it tomorrow. People who drink and smoke started by thinking that they would one day quit their habit. Too late they discovered it wasn't as easy as they had imagined. Youth is the best time to give one's life to God.

It's a fallacy to think that it's easy to change one's lifestyle at the eleventh hour. I think of Max, a young man whose life slid into drinking and sexual immorality. After years of living life in the fast lane, he contracted a terminal sexually transmitted disease. A number of times he was visited by people from the church to encourage him to give his life to God. As he lay on his deathbed, he commented that the only images that passed through his mind were those of beer and women!

It is interesting that among the children of Jacob Joseph's life is given prominence. In fact, our story begins this way: 'This is the

Victory *through* DEFEAT

account of Jacob', but then it suddenly shifts to Joseph. The selection of Joseph is not arbitrary. Of all Jacob's children, Joseph is the closest to the heart of God. At an early age he absorbs the spiritual teachings of his father and seeks the way of God. Many years later, as Jacob is about to die, he gathers his children to bless them. It is Joseph who receives the most praise. Jacob says more about Joseph than any of his other sons. And even though it is not through his lineage that the Saviour is born, he of all Jacob's children lives the most fruitful and fulfilling life. Joseph's life reads stranger than fiction. All of this happens because he gives himself unreservedly into the Master Designer's hands at an early age. He attains greatness that is unequalled and unparalleled by his own brothers.

The typical modern young person would find the kind of life Joseph and his brothers were engaged in quite boring and time wasting. Yet the truth that confronts us shows that life is meant to be practical. Satan in a bid to trap youngsters has brought all kinds of games to lure them from a life of contemplation and active engagement in useful activities into computer games, the Internet, television watching and other such empty occupations. Yet real life cannot be lived like that by the majority of people. Those who live in palaces and Hollywood are in the minority. It is true that most people are not farmers today. They are not nomadic shepherds by occupation. However, what's important in this passage is the principle. The teaching of practical skills at an early age is important in forming a spiritual character. As a young man, Jesus worked with his father Joseph at the carpenter's trade.

The home where Joseph grew up was rather complicated, socially speaking. With four women in charge, the children often grouped themselves according to their birth mothers. It was just natural for those cliques to exist. Despite the fact that we have one

1   *The growing-up years*

heavenly Father, it is not uncommon to identify ourselves according to our nationality or social standing. During the soccer World Cup of 2004 I was in Kampala, Uganda, on church business. The afternoon Senegal won against world champions France was the high day of the tournament in Africa. I still remember the explosion of excitement and applause when Senegal scored the lone goal that humiliated the French team. To many Africans, that titanic soccer encounter was a case of Black versus White.

The other day I watched a boxing match between Zambia's Esther Phiri, Women's International Boxing Federation super flyweight champion, and Monica Petrova of Bulgaria. I have to admit that being Zambian I was anxious to see the result go in Esther's favour. And even though I am reluctant to admit this, I was happy and relieved when Esther successfully defended her title on a unanimous decision.

The important thing to remember in the story of Joseph and his brothers is that even though they came from four different mothers, they had one father – Jacob. On the basis of coming from one father these boys were given the chance to live and work together successfully. At the spiritual level, God's people are given the chance to dwell together. We may hail from different nations and backgrounds – male and female, young and old, educated and uneducated, rich and poor – yet we may live in harmony as children of one Father. In the Lord's Prayer, Jesus teaches his disciples to begin in this way: '*Our* Father . . .' (Matthew 6:9). The Lord makes it clear that he is not simply a Father to George Mwansa, a Zambian from Africa. He is also a Father to many millions of people from different parts of the world. These others then become George's brothers and sisters. John put it well when he wrote: 'To all who received him, to those who believed in his name, he gave the right to become children of God' (John 1:12). And as Paul reminds us: 'There is neither Jew nor Greek, slave nor free, male nor female, for you are all one in Christ Jesus.' (Galatians 3:28.)

Victory *through* DEFEAT

As God's people we must be united. Yet all too often we are not. I came into the family of God from a race of black Africans. I was born in Zambia among the Bemba-speaking people. When I became united with God's people, I must admit that all too often I thought, spoke and lived not as one who had become a child of God. Yet these outward trappings must not define who I am now. I am now supposed to be a born-again person whose concerns and interests are those of my new Father, God. The apostle Paul through his epistle to the Romans reminds us: 'Clothe yourselves with the Lord Jesus Christ' (13:14). 'For all of you who were baptised into Christ have clothed yourselves with Christ' (Galatians 3:27). What therefore defines me first and foremost is not my skin colour, the language I speak or the country I hail from; rather, it is the new status I have acquired in Christ Jesus. I now have a new country – Heaven. 'Our citizenship,' the Bible tells us, 'is in heaven' (see Philippians 3:20). Having acquired this new citizenship, I must begin to learn its language and all its other requirements.

I do hope that my young readers and friends can also see in this story that force we refer to as peer pressure. Because all my friends see it, say it and do it this way, I must also see it, say it and do it the same way. That's peer pressure. The pressure to conform is real. But young Joseph gives an example not only to youth but to adults that all can be independent thinkers. He had seen what his brothers were doing when they were out tending animals. His brothers ganged up on him, poked fun at and often ridiculed him. But what mattered to Joseph was God's view of things. He always remembered the beautiful lessons of obedience his father taught them. The young people, especially, must remember that what matters is what God says about something, not what their peers say.

Young Mulenga grew up in a home where God was worshipped.

1   *The growing-up years*

Her parents taught her from an early age to love and fear God as Maker and Redeemer. She was a promising child in a family that was well knit and united. Mulenga had a pretty face and a well-shaped figure. Her parents expected great things of her. In high school she was confronted with many of the peer-pressure issues young people face. Every one of her friends had a boyfriend. It was the in thing. She did not have one because she just wasn't interested. The pressure started to mount up from her friends who could not understand how a pretty girl like her could live without a boyfriend. At first she resisted the pressure, but as time went on she began to think that there could be truth in what her friends were saying. Why hadn't she found someone to love? Could it be that there was something wrong with her? Then she met a boy from another school who liked to hang around her each time there was an opportunity. She didn't like him at all. She confessed that there was no trace of love in her heart for that boy. But the pressure of having someone she could introduce as a boyfriend had mounted to unmanageable proportions. As she continued to see the boy, she eventually began to tolerate him. One day towards the end of her school career, she found herself and her guy in a compromising situation. He forced himself on her and she became pregnant.

The desire to be like others is real, but so is God. At that early age when young people rarely care about what God says, Joseph proves that one doesn't have to be a sheep. Joseph had determined in his heart early in life that he would allow only the God of his fathers to be the Ruler of his life. He closed the door to self, Satan and the world of peer pressure. The result was a pure life that brought him close to God.

Joseph also proves that greatness does not depend upon our being in the majority. He reminds us that life must always be viewed from the standpoint of Heaven. 'If God is for us, who can be against us?' (Romans 8:31.) As God's people we must always remember that those who are with us are more than those who are against us.

Victory *through* **DEFEAT**

(See 2 Kings 6:16.) One person plus God is always in the majority, in spite of all the odds. The rightness of an issue must never be determined by numbers, but by what God says. Even if a thousand people in real life and another thousand on television and the Internet tell you that sex outside of marriage is OK, it does not make it right. True, God wants to save everyone. In fact, Christ's sacrifice on the Cross was for all humanity. But one has to choose to be on the side of God for that sacrifice to be of meaning and benefit. And, by the way, with God it's not really about numbers. You will be interested to know that during the flood only eight believing people were saved. And during the fire that fell on Sodom and Gomorrah only three people escaped death. Indeed, as Jesus put it, 'Many are called, but few are chosen.' (Matthew 22:14, KJV.) Therefore we would do well to 'Enter through the narrow gate. For wide is the gate and broad is the road that leads to destruction, and many enter through it. But small is the gate and narrow the road that leads to life, and only a few find it.' (Matthew 7:13-14.)

It is rather fascinating that the setting of Joseph's story begins with a confrontation: his brothers versus Joseph. Joseph brings to his father a bad report about his brothers, making them unhappy and cross with him. From the outset, a picture emerges that reminds us of the two forces at war in this life: the force of good and the force of evil. The evil forces seem almost always to take an upper hand. They appear to be many and always set to destroy the good. Life is indeed a drama between the seemingly insignificant forces of good and the seemingly powerful forces of evil. The voice from the camp of the evil one seems to be louder, stronger and bolder. It beckons us to do things our own way, the way of the world or Satan's way. It uses powerful means at its disposal: radio, television, newspapers, the Internet and a host of other mass-media outlets. On the other

hand is the seemingly weak voice of the small force of those who belong to the Almighty One. This is the group of Joseph, the group to which we must all belong as God's children.

Victory *through* **DEFEAT**

Chapter 2

Jacob's indulgent love and Joseph's dreams

'Now Israel loved Joseph more than any of his other sons, because he had been born to him in his old age; and he made a richly ornamented robe for him. When his brothers saw that their father loved him more than any of them, they hated him and could not speak a kind word to him.

'Joseph had a dream, and when he told it to his brothers, they hated him all the more. He said to them, "Listen to this dream I had: We were binding sheaves of grain out in the field when suddenly my sheaf rose and stood upright, while your sheaves gathered around mine and bowed down to it."

'His brothers said to him, "Do you intend to reign over us? Will you actually rule us?" And they hated him all the more because of his dream and what he had said.

'Then he had another dream, and he told it to his brothers. "Listen," he said, "I had another dream, and this time the sun and moon and eleven stars were bowing down to me."

'When he told his father as well as his brothers, his father rebuked him and said, "What is this dream you had? Will your mother and I and your brothers actually come and bow down to the ground before you?" His brothers were jealous of him, but his father kept the matter in mind.' (Genesis 37:3-11.)

2 *Jacob's indulgent love and Joseph's dreams*

Joseph's life at home was not a particularly easy one, owing in part to his father's love that placed him above the other children. This indulgent love made him a target of jealousy and envy. Joseph's life of purity and the dreams he shared which also placed him above everyone at home did not help matters. His was, undoubtedly, a lonely life. However, it helped to know that his father loved him. Joseph could thus survive in a home of strained relationships. More important than his father's love was Joseph's living relationship with God.

The subject of dreams is a tricky one. I have met several people whose lives are to some degree guided by dreams and visions. Some of the things they dream about often come true, while others don't. Many of these good people believe strongly that their dreams and visions come from God. A man I know was once approached by a woman and told that she had been shown in a dream by God that he was to be her husband. The man was a widower, but unknown to that lady, he already had a steady relationship with another woman. To complicate matters, the man said that he had no love for the 'dream' girl. Moreover, why would God communicate in such a dramatic way only to the woman, leaving the man completely in the dark?

The other day someone told me he had a gift of prophecy from the Lord. 'God often shows me scenes in the lives of other people that almost always reflect reality. Some scenes are shown to me in dreams and others just come like live clips,' he said. Another person said: 'My dreams are usually very vivid and often come true. For example, the other day I dreamed that we had been given a pay rise at our workplace and, sure enough, the following day it happened just like that.' Still another said: 'Usually when I have bad dreams like relatives being sick or dead, it happens that someone from the family will have an accident, get sick or even die.'

I have no doubt that these people are sincerely telling the truth. That they have had such dreams, I don't doubt. However, the big

Victory *through* **DEFEAT**

question each of these people must seek to answer is, 'Who is the source of all these things?' Is it possible that someone other than God could be communicating to them? Or are they the result of heavy meals late at night? Mostly dreams are just dances of disorder reflecting the unresolved issues of our conscious lives.

In the passage under consideration it is worth noting that all the dreams Joseph had came from the Lord. It's important to remember this point, because many people have been misguided by strange spirits through dreams which come true quite often, but occasionally do not.

And when we look at dreams and visions in a secondary sense, I expect each of us has things we dream about, visions we have about the future. These are often strong desires and impressions of what we hope we can do or be some day. We must be aware that there are always four sources from which these dreams and visions can come: our corrupted self, the world, Satan and God. Among these sources only that of God is safe. Visions from God will relate to his plans for the world. Unless these dreams and visions and ambitions are from God, they act only to destroy us. It is, therefore, absolutely critical that we know in every situation whether we are being driven by self, the world, Satan or God.

In the case before us, we have an example of dreams coming from God. Dreams that come from God – whether they are actual or simply strong desires and impressions – keep us on the narrow path that leads to Heaven. On the other hand, those that come from Satan, self and the world keep us on the broad path that leads to hell.

And still on the subject of dreams, visions and ambitions, we must be careful that we don't necessarily share these publicly just because they come from the Lord. Often it is more prudent to keep matters to ourselves and simply proceed on the basis of what God is

2 Jacob's indulgent love and Joseph's dreams

saying than to share things with every Jim and Jack we meet. People may pour water on those dreams and dampen our spirit, in some cases even discouraging us to the point of our giving up. Being incapable of hating anyone, Joseph could not envisage his brothers' hating him. He had travelled seventy-five miles to find them as he loved them. Joseph would have acted more wisely by simply keeping the dreams to himself. These dreams may have simply been intended to reveal to him the glorious future that awaited him in the light of the tragic events that were soon to follow. Sharing them with his siblings was like pouring fuel on a fire that was already burning. Perhaps the human tendency to boast is the reason why God so rarely uses dreams and visions these days.

But given that God allowed it to happen that way, what are some of the lessons we learn? One lesson is that what God shows to us, exciting though it may be, does not necessarily make it welcome to others. As a matter of fact it may just fuel their jealousy and hatred. Jesus came to our world on a mission to save us. It was a mission and vision without parallel. At Jesus' baptism, bystanders heard the voice of God in Heaven saying: 'This is my Son, whom I love; with him I am well pleased.' (Matthew 3:17.) In another place in the same book God said this about his Son: 'Here is my servant whom I have chosen, the one I love, in whom I delight; I will put my Spirit on him, and he will proclaim justice to the nations.' (12:18.) In both the mission of Joseph and that of Jesus, the unction from on high had the great purpose of saving others. Joseph was lifted above others in order to serve and save them; so was Jesus. But in the case of both Joseph and Jesus their mission or vision became the cause of their persecution and, for Jesus, even death.

I found it interesting that though Joseph's brothers hated him when he shared his dreams, they listened. One would have thought that immediately Joseph opened his mouth, they would all have dismissed him or just walked away. However, instead of dismissing him, they paid attention to what he had to say. There is something

Victory *through* DEFEAT

compelling about God's people. While they may be hated in this world, God grants them power to live and speak so they can be seen and heard. Is it not strange that in a world that's ruled by Satan, God's people could even have a right to say something? Indeed it shows that God is truly at work. Viewed from this angle, the words of our Lord in Matthew 28:18-20 take on a new meaning and make important reading: 'All authority in heaven and on earth has been given to me. Therefore go and make disciples of all nations, baptising them in the name of the Father and of the Son and of the Holy Spirit, and teaching them to obey everything I have commanded you. And surely I am with you always, to the very end of the age.' The wicked are somehow compelled to listen to the message of salvation and many of them even believe it and are saved.

3 *Chapter 3*
Joseph parts from his father

'Now his brothers had gone to graze their father's flocks near Shechem, and Israel said to Joseph, "As you know, your brothers are grazing the flocks near Shechem. Come, I am going to send you to them." "Very well," he replied. So he said to him, "Go and see if all is well with your brothers and with the flocks, and bring word back to me." Then he sent him off from the Valley of Hebron.' (Genesis 37:12-14.)

Those of us who have read this story know that by agreeing to undertake this trip Joseph will not see his father for a very long time. Secretly we even wish that he had disobeyed the word of his father. Disobedience would have helped both Joseph and his father to avoid separation. But Joseph did not know what was going to happen to him. As an obedient child he did what was not only right in the eyes of his father but God as well. 'Children, obey your parents in the Lord, for this is right. "Honour your father and mother" – which is the first commandment with a promise – "that it may go well with you and that you may enjoy long life on the earth." ' (Ephesians 6:1-3.) Yet we must remember the paradoxical nature of God's Word. Obedience to God's commands often has seemingly disastrous consequences.

Because of his obedience in preaching the Word of God, Humberto Noble Alexander suffered twenty-two years in Cuban prisons. Obedience to God caused the three Hebrew young men to be cast into the fiery furnace. Daniel was thrown into the lions' den because of his obedience to the God of Heaven. Obedience to the Word of God caused John the Baptist to be thrown into prison and ultimately lose his life there. However, doing the right thing is the

Victory *through* **DEFEAT**

right thing to do no matter what results this may bring. We make this preamble because we have read this story and we know that Joseph's conversation with his father at this time will be their last in Canaan.

Joseph did not know that that would be his last sight of his father for over twenty years. His father, too, had no idea that in a matter of days he would begin to mourn the loss of his beloved son. And that's the tragic thing about life. It is unpredictable. In fact, the only predictable thing about life is that it is unpredictable. Often it will take only a simple decision to plunge one's life into the abyss of trauma, stress and depression. Unfortunately, even the good decisions we make in life bring about disastrous consequences. My late wife, Martha, was travelling with my brother Alex to attend the funeral of my sister Mwape when both died in a road traffic accident near Serenje, Zambia. But God's Word gives this assurance: 'Even though I walk through the valley of the shadow of death, I will fear no evil, for you are with me.' (Psalms 23:4.)

We commend Joseph here for agreeing to find his brothers, despite the sibling rivalries that existed between them. They were his brothers, after all. Indeed, the best way to deal with family jealousies and misunderstandings is not to participate in them. We cannot solve family feuds using the tit-for-tat, eye-for-eye, tooth-for-tooth methods. Love is the only way. 'Love your enemies and pray for those who persecute you' (Matthew 5:44), Jesus said. Joseph could have chosen to live a sulky and bitter life in that atmosphere that was tainted with jealousy and hatred, but the force of love is the only power that can sustain a person under such circumstances.

Joseph travelled a long distance just to see how his brothers were doing. That's love. Love, by its very nature, gives and seeks the good of others. Love is not about studying how love operates, but

3   *Joseph parts from his father*

doing what it requires. If we love people, we shall not just talk about it; we shall visit them, help them and do other sacrificial things that love often demands.

In this one act of Joseph we also see the story of redemption replayed. God, looking into the interests of his wayward children, sent his one and only Son to a cruel world that would not receive him and would later kill him.

Israel says to his son Joseph: 'Go and see if all is well with your brothers. . . .' From his perspective, all are his children, despite the fact that they have come from four different mothers. It is important to highlight this point again because of the distortions brought about by sin. Though believers may come from different countries and their skin colour may be different, the fact is that they are all children of the same Father – God.

One time while on a church trip to some African country with a friend and colleague from Zambia, I was surprised by the strange introduction given him before a huge gathering of church members. After the announcement of who he was and what position he held in the organisation, the audience was told that he hailed from Zambia. Ordinarily, that would have been sufficient, but another statement was added: 'This man also holds an American citizenship.' Later on I asked my friend in private what relevancy that statement of holding an American citizenship held. He told me, as he smiled with obvious bemusement and discomfort, that among some people when you are from America it raises your status. It saddened him as well to think that in the eyes of some people he needed the American 'prop' to be raised to a higher level in their estimation. No doubt America, the dominant nation, is the most powerful, but her citizens are by no means superior to those coming from the other nations of the world.

In my family there were originally five boys and two girls. At the time of my writing this manuscript two are dead. The eldest, a medical doctor, is of medium build. The second, a primary school teacher, is tall. I, the third, am of medium height, while the one who

Victory *through* DEFEAT

comes after me, a secondary school teacher, is tall. The girl who comes after my young brother is small, and what some people would describe as slim. A few in the family are light skinned while others are dark. We all live in different places and do different things. However, notwithstanding our differences, we are all children of Mr Zachariah Mwansa. (Our mother is dead.)

It is the same in the household of faith. We are different but children of one Father.

Tadao Shimeon is a Japanese man who once served as communication director for the Asia Pacific Division while I served in the same capacity for the Eastern Africa Division in the 90s. We met in several forums in Brazil, USA, Canada and England. Tadao is a cool, down-to-earth guy. He has a very warm and approachable personality. I remember our ride one time through the streets of London on one of those double-decker buses that cater for tourists. We talked and enjoyed each other's company as though we were children of one father and mother. Now, let's face the facts. I would not be far from telling the truth by observing that the world of technology is one in which our Japanese friends are at the front of the queue. What can one think of in the area of modern technology that cannot be made in Japan? Yet this guy, Tadao, though he is much older, of different origin and colour and hails from the most technologically advanced nation of the world, has no trace of arrogance, bigotry or any other such negative trait. It actually took me years to learn he has an earned doctorate.

An individual who bases his superiority on his skin colour or the nation he hails from simply reveals his lack of self-esteem. He is also ignorant of the creation and redemption stories. Equally, the one who feels inferior on account of his skin colour or national origin or any other class barrier simply reveals his ignorance of the two great

3 *Joseph parts from his father*

stories of creation and redemption. It was the same price the Father paid to save an American and an Armenian. 'For God so loved the world that he gave his one and only Son, that whoever believes in him shall not perish but have eternal life.' (John 3:16.)

Victory *through* DEFEAT

Chapter 4

Joseph arrives at Shechem

'When Joseph arrived at Shechem, a man found him wandering around in the fields and asked him, "What are you looking for?" He replied, "I'm looking for my brothers. Can you tell me where they are grazing their flocks?" "They have moved on from here," the man answered. "I heard them say, 'Let's go to Dothan.' " So Joseph went after his brothers and found them near Dothan.' (Genesis 37:14-17.)

Upon arrival at Shechem, Joseph did not find his brothers. But God who had already gone before him sent a man who had information that would lead Joseph to the whereabouts of his brothers. God is indeed an ever-present help in time of need. His promise never to leave us alone or to forsake us is encouraging. We don't need to own communication gadgets like the Internet or cell phones in order to call for help. The poorest person can have the easiest access to God. Indeed, there is no such thing as getting stranded for he is always there for us. When it appears that we are stranded, it is because God is working one of his mysterious purposes out – something of which we are unaware. And, in any case, everything works together for good to those who love him (see Romans 8:28).

Interestingly, the conversation is opened not by Joseph who is desperate but by someone who is not involved. God often works like

that. He will bring people along our path to help us in ways that baffle us. Perhaps out of concern for the seventeen-year-old boy travelling alone, the man asks what Joseph is looking for. And very interestingly he asks just the kind of question a young man in a predicament would be happy to hear: 'What are you looking for?'

My friend Nyasha Musvosvi shared with me an experience that illustrates this point well. Musvosvi and his family had travelled from Zimbabwe their home country to Johannesburg, South Africa. When they arrived in Johannesburg his son got sick and needed immediate medical attention. Musvosvi took him to a private clinic, but before he could see the doctor, a man he did not know asked him where he was from. 'Zimbabwe,' he said. The man told him that because he was a foreigner he would have to pay a large sum of money at that private clinic. He suggested that they should follow him to a government hospital.

At the government hospital the man took Musvosvi's boy and explained to the staff that the sick boy whose name was Thomas Ndhlilose (fictitious name that he mentioned to get the needed help) was his sister's son and was visiting him but had forgotten the identity document. The boy was treated free of charge!

Because so often we take the blessings of God for granted, we probably are not even thinking about the fact that Joseph arrived at Shechem safely. We must remind ourselves that there is an enemy who roams about seeking someone to devour by whatever means. If he can't devour us spiritually, he will seek to devour us physically. Satan is angry with those who don't take his orders. People like Joseph are in danger. Satan knows that this boy Joseph has an important role to play. It was therefore a miracle that Joseph arrived safely not only at Shechem but Dothan.

Joseph, unlike Cain, accepted the fact that he was his brothers' keeper. He could therefore look after their interests. His brothers had moved from where they were expected to be found to some other place. Joseph could have easily called off the search at that

Victory *through* DEFEAT

point but he did not. He had an obligation both to them as well as to his father. God wants his children to have this same caring mindset. But not only does he ask us to have this loving attitude towards one another; God wants us to look for those who are lost that they, too, may be a part of the family. Though the people out there may slight and despitefully use us, we are to remember that they are our brothers and sisters. Their nationalities, colour of skin and language are simply artificial things. We are all children of one Father. One day we shall live together in Heaven and the new earth.

Yes, Joseph could have called off his trip after learning that his brothers had left for Dothan – fifteen miles away from where he stood. He could have gone back to relay the news he received from the stranger he met at Shechem but that would have been an incomplete report. Joseph, like the Good Samaritan, was willing to go the second mile for the sake of locating his brothers and taking back a concrete report to his father. God doesn't want his people to do half-baked work. The work of saving souls is always fraught with great obstacles and sacrifice. It took Jesus' great sacrifice to save this lost world. He accomplished his mission to the full. He went beyond Gethsemane – all the way to the Cross and died the death that was ours. Joseph, too, went after his brothers all the way and found them at Dothan. Undoubtedly he felt exhausted, but for the sake of his brothers and father he was willing to do it.

Jacob trusted his son Joseph with the responsibility which he, himself, could have accomplished well. God could finish his work of saving sinners in a moment. He could cause millions of conversions where there are few today. Entire populations could be aroused to their need of a Saviour by his miraculous powers in a matter of seconds. Remember, in one story Peter had laboured the whole night trying to catch fish and couldn't get even a single one. Then Jesus told Peter to 'put out into the deep water, and let down the nets for a catch.' (Luke 5:4.) We are told that 'When they had done so, they caught such a large number of fish that their nets began to break.' (Luke 5:6.) God can indeed do it alone in a grand fashion, but he wants us to be a part of the programme. What an honour this is for us!

Victory *through* **DEFEAT**

Chapter 5

Joseph is confronted by his brothers

'But they saw him in the distance, and before he reached them, they plotted to kill him. "Here comes that dreamer!" they said to each other. "Come now, let's kill him and throw him into one of these cisterns and say that a ferocious animal devoured him. Then we'll see what comes of his dreams." When Reuben heard this, he tried to rescue him from their hands. "Let's not take his life," he said. "Don't shed any blood. Throw him into this cistern here in the desert, but don't lay a hand on him." Reuben said this to rescue him from them and take him back to his father.' (Genesis 37:18-22.)

Lest we forget, those who quickly hatch this plan are blood brothers. The proverb, 'Blood is thicker than water,' may, after all, not be always as true and relevant as people like to put it – at least in this particular situation. We are reminded of the words of our Lord Jesus: 'A man's enemies will be the members of his own household' (Matthew 10:36). It seems that in spite of what we often say, the family edifice that's based on blood ties does not stand on strong pillars of support.

Thus it becomes important for God to create a new family that is not based on blood ties. John says it well: 'To all who received him, to those who believed in his name, he gave the right to become children of God – children born not of natural descent, nor of human

5   *Joseph is confronted by his brothers*

decision or a husband's will, but born of God.' (John 1:12, 13.) And Jesus himself clarifies the important question of who his brother, mother and sister are: 'Whoever does the will of my Father in heaven is my brother and sister and mother.' (Matthew 12:50.) This new family is made possible through Jesus. Members of one blood family are, of course, not excluded from becoming a part of this great family. All who believe in Christ become members.

This episode illustrates well how light and darkness just can't co-exist. Joseph had a different spirit from those of his brothers. The two parties were like oil and water or clay and iron mixed together. Paul, the apostle to the Gentiles, reminds us: 'What fellowship can light have with darkness?' (2 Corinthians 6:14.)

But there is also another lesson here. Paul says: 'Everyone who wants to live a godly life in Christ Jesus will be persecuted' (2 Timothy 3:12).

From earlier passages that we read, we came across statements such as: 'They hated him all the more,' 'His brothers were jealous of him.' We never took those statements seriously. We concluded that they were just petty sibling rivalries. But when we read here that these brothers are prepared to kill him, we begin to see how even the smallest seed of sin can grow into a giant plant. We are reminded again of the words of our Lord Jesus: 'You have heard that it was said to the people long ago, "Do not murder, and anyone who murders will be subject to judgement." But I tell you that anyone who is angry with his brother will be subject to judgement.' (Matthew 5:21-22.)

The problem, as with all things with us humans, is the heart. Our deeds are merely signs and symptoms of what already exists in the heart. There is therefore a need for a new heart which only God can give, a heart of flesh and not stone. There is a need to be born again. That's the starting point, not to attack or try to manipulate behaviour. Judging by their behaviour, we see that Joseph's brothers needed new hearts.

Victory *through* DEFEAT

As Joseph's brothers hatch their evil plot, we are reminded of the evil in evil men that seems to be aroused to great passion by the good in good men. The brothers of Joseph seemed to be OK until Joseph appeared. The presence of Joseph was always a thorn in their flesh. Evil secretly admires good but won't admit it. And, because it stands in an inferior position, evil often flexes its muscles in the face of good to punish it. Evil wants to show that it is stronger and can subdue good.

Viewed from our blurred human perspective, Joseph appears to be alone. He is defenceless and powerless against his ten brothers. But is Joseph really alone? No, for though he cannot see them, Joseph is surrounded by angels from Heaven. We must remember that there are many things we cannot see that are nevertheless real. Surrounding us, for example, on every corner are airwaves transmitting millions of messages to radios, walkie-talkies, televisions and phones.

The fact that we don't see them does not mean they are not there. Joseph appeared to be alone but he was not. He was in the majority. This is a point that we easily forget. Those who are with us – so long as we are with God – are more than those who are against us and infinitely stronger. If Joseph will be harmed in this story, we must remember that his position will become stronger and his enemies' weaker. God has gone into Joseph's future, ahead of time, and knows what will happen.

Joseph's brothers are now in a position where they can use 'number' power to decide his fate. What will they do with that power? Will they honour God by doing the right thing or will they misuse it and abuse that power? Often God puts us into positions of authority – advantageous positions to see how we will use that authority. As parents, teachers, administrators and so on, how have

5   *Joseph is confronted by his brothers*

we used that power? In the case of Joseph's brothers, they decide that they will kill him.

In the evil camp the end always justifies the means. 'Let's kill him,' they say, 'then we will see what comes of his dreams.' The question is: can this action be justified in the eyes of God? The answer is an obvious no. But that's how things are always done in the camp of the wicked. If killing will accomplish the job, then so be it. If cheating will do it, so be it. From this bad example we are warned about the terrible consequences of living our lives outside of God. We shall continue to drift until even the unthinkable becomes thinkable.

'We will kill him,' they confer, 'and we will then report that a ferocious animal devoured him.' Killing will lead to another sin – lying! No wonder James 2:10, 11 argues: 'For whoever keeps the whole law and yet stumbles at just one point is guilty of breaking all of it. For he who said, "Do not commit adultery," also said, "Do not murder." If you do not commit adultery but do commit murder, you have become a law-breaker.'

As those people were planning their wicked act, they had no idea that one day someone would write about them and make their story an open book for all to read. They thought that that act would be kept a secret. But their story has been read and reread for several thousands of years by millions of people around the world. Are the things we do in secret really secret? The Bible says that 'Nothing in all creation is hidden from God's sight. Everything is uncovered and laid bare before the eyes of him to whom we must give account.' (Hebrews 4:13.)

God gave us eyes to see so we would not walk like blind people. But do we use them for good or evil purposes? When Joseph's brothers saw him, they plotted to kill him. On the other hand, Joseph used his eyes for a good purpose, to look for his brothers so he could know how they were doing. How do we use members of our bodies? Is it to glorify self or God? Paul bids us to employ them for holy purposes: 'Do not let any part of your body become a tool of

Victory *through* DEFEAT

wickedness, to be used for sinning. Instead give yourselves completely to God since you have been given new life. And use your whole body as a tool to do what is right for the glory of God.' (Romans 6:13, NLT.)

By exerting his influence as the eldest in the family, Reuben was used by God to prevent the killing of Joseph. Joseph's time to leave the world had not yet come. No matter what the devil could do, the arrow of death could not strike Joseph. Our lives are truly in the hands of God. Not long ago I had a phone call from an acquaintance living in a faraway country. I can't remember what we were talking about but I found myself asking him when he was planning to visit home. 'Me visiting home? Never! I don't want my relatives to bewitch me!' I responded by reminding him that his life was in God's hands.

'You are indestructible until God says otherwise,' I said.

'Yeah, that may be true, but I also believe that witchcraft works,' he said, being unconvinced.

'True,' I countered. 'Witchcraft is there, but as a child of God if you had to die because of witchcraft, God would have to allow it. Otherwise, nothing could harm you.'

Joseph's brothers had the power to kill him, but his time was not up. God made sure it didn't happen.

From Reuben we learn something worth remembering. Each of us in certain ways has some influence in helping the cause of God or some individual out there. Each day that we live affords us an opportunity to live for God so that some soul may be blessed or helped to move from the kingdom of darkness to the kingdom of light. Reuben – hitherto unknown for any particular strength of character – has a part to play in saving Joseph from death.

Strangely, the one who comes to the rescue of Joseph is not an angel or indeed the 'right kind of a person'. On the contrary, it is

5   *Joseph is confronted by his brothers*

someone from the enemy's camp. Reuben like the other brothers did not like Joseph at all. How do we then explain his sudden shift of mind to become the one who rescues Joseph from their hands? God need not always have the right person to accomplish his will. It is not always the case that God's men must be there in order for God's will to prevail. This situation teaches us that God is in control at all times. We don't have to have the right man in the right office for things to move favourably for us. God is sufficient in any and every given situation. God has the ability to use even those who are not on his side to accomplish his will if he so wills.

Victory *through* DEFEAT

Chapter 6

Joseph receives a rude reception

'So when Joseph came to his brothers, they stripped him of his robe – the richly ornamented robe he was wearing – and they took him and threw him into the cistern. Now the cistern was empty; there was no water in it.' (Genesis 37:23, 24.)

Joseph was undoubtedly tired but glad that he had at long last located his brothers. But what a welcome it was! How ungrateful he thought they were. He had walked the long distance out of concern for them and that was the 'reward' he was getting! Like Jesus, he came to his own and his own did not receive him. We are reminded here, as in many places of Scripture, that pursuing the interests of our brethren does not automatically lead to praise and good treatment. We had better learn quickly the principle of doing right for right's own sake. And when we pass through this kind of setback we must remember that our Lord passed through it as well. His own people whom he had come to save did not just reject him but they went on to kill him!

Thank God that while everything else can be taken away from us by our enemies, there is one thing at least they cannot take away: our relationship with God. Joseph's richly ornamented robe was stripped off him, never again to be seen or worn by him. Interestingly, God did not prevent that from happening. But God

would not allow Joseph's enemy brothers to take away the relationship – God's personal presence. In the final analysis, the only thing that really matters is God's presence in our lives.

What was Joseph thinking about as he sat in the empty cistern unable to help himself? Whatever was going through his mind, God knew. Isn't it encouraging to know that God knows our thoughts and all the pain we go through? But does it really make any difference that God knows? Yes. How? The fact that God knows means everything. If God knows about it, he will do something about it. Listen to these words of our Lord Jesus: 'If you sinful people know how to give good gifts to your children, how much more will your heavenly Father give good gifts to those who ask him?' (Matthew 7:11, NLT.) God will allow only what he knows will ultimately work for our good. And lest we forget, with the temptation also comes the way out. (See 1 Corinthians 10:13.)

In this bad situation, Joseph's brothers have an opportunity to see themselves as they really have become, tainted with jealousy and hatred. If they are wise, they will learn something. Our evil deeds can lead to wake-up calls. I am personally thankful that God gives us opportunities to reform. Peter denies his Lord three times. God could abandon him. But he does not do that. That denial becomes a learning experience for Peter, giving him a glimpse of who he truly is. He has two options: to run away from God in despair or be drawn to God in repentance. God can use our fallings and failings as a means to draw us to himself. In this sense then, paradoxical though it may sound, falling can become a means to rising. This is why we must never be quick to condemn those who have fallen. We must, instead, pray that God will use the bad that happens to them as a means to bring them back.

Through Judah Messiah would be born. We must be thankful that God sees the whole span of human life – from beginning to end. We must be thankful that he is a compassionate, merciful, kind and loving Father. I praise God, for I see in these brothers my own

Victory *through* **DEFEAT**

picture. I see in them also a picture of how God looks at me. Yes, even though I am far from being who God wants me to be, he will continue to love and work with me until his purposes for me are all accomplished. Praise God!

7

Chapter 7

Joseph's brothers agree to sell him

'As they sat down to eat their meal, they looked up and saw a caravan of Ishmaelites coming from Gilead. Their camels were loaded with spices, balm and myrrh, and they were on their way to take them down to Egypt. Judah said to his brothers, "What will we gain if we kill our brother and cover up his blood? Come, let's sell him to the Ishmaelites and not lay our hands on him; after all, he is our brother, our own flesh and blood." His brothers agreed. So when the Midianite merchants came by, his brothers pulled Joseph up out of the cistern and sold him for twenty shekels of silver to the Ishmaelites, who took him to Egypt.' (Genesis 37:25-28.)

As this decision is made, no one has any idea as to the impact of the soon-to-be-taken action. The decision is made casually with little reflection as to its consequences. But a just-like-that kind of decision changed the course of history. A rash action can have serious consequences. To Eve, the question of eating the forbidden fruit might have probably appeared small, but it changed the course of earth's history.

A young woman tells the story of how she agreed to host a male friend at her apartment. He had lied that he didn't have money for transport to his destination and was therefore asking if he could spend the night at her place. They were good friends, but the young lady felt a bit uncomfortable at the idea. But then she liked him and he was a nice guy. He was known in the Adventist community as a dynamic lay-preacher. The young lady agreed, though her conscience continued to flash red all night. That night, in the woman's one-bedroom apartment, the inevitable happened. The two slept together. From that single encounter, three months later the woman

Victory *through* DEFEAT

tested HIV positive. Our safety lies only in obeying what God says.

The mistreatment of Joseph scenario has been repeated millions of times among brethren. Committees sit and decide cases, sometimes on the basis of misinformation, half-truths and distortions. For reasons best known to Satan, somehow we, as God's people, have not learned to deal with one another lovingly and kindly. The Bible is so clear about this that we don't even need to repeat it here. While it is true that we like talking and writing about love, we rarely practise it among ourselves. Judah says to the others, 'This guy Joseph is our brother; let's not kill him; let's just banish him from our presence so that he may no longer bother us with his dreams and good-boy behaviour.' Judah seems to suggest something that is common among us, too: we don't want to work with a guy who is too often an obstacle in our way. We will do everything to get rid of such a one.

But what a terrible coincidence this is. It just so happened that Reuben, the oldest brother who would have refused to go along with Judah's plan, was not there. And those who were prepared to buy Joseph had just arrived on the scene! Lord, why do things happen this way? Why is the one you love placed in this kind of situation where everything just goes to work perfectly against him? We know that through a series of 'unfortunate' circumstances Joseph would later become prime minister in the land of his exile, Egypt. And the lesson here is that in spite of the multiple forces of evil that may confront and seek to destroy us at every turn, God will work out something positive for us.

Yes, if we did not know the end of this story, we could think of God as a Father who doesn't really love his children, for how could he allow Joseph to be so systematically and methodically trapped? We could also think of God as someone who does not really know the

Joseph's brothers agree to sell him

future; someone who is as taken by surprise by events as we all are. We could easily view God as someone who does not really have a grip on what happens, notwithstanding his claims in his Word. And this view of God is what's, unfortunately, so strong when we are terrorised by the evil one. In those moments when it appears that God has abandoned us to the mercy of the enemy, the view that God doesn't really care, he is not powerful and strong as he claims, he is not as understanding and loving as he says – that view becomes too often our main preoccupation.

God gave us the gift of speech for noble reasons. Writing to the Ephesians, Paul says: 'Do not let any unwholesome talk come out of your mouths, but only what is helpful for building others up according to their needs, that it may benefit those who listen.' (Ephesians 4:29.) Judah's suggestion to his brothers that Joseph be sold is an example of how not to use the gift of speech. Judah persuaded his brothers to act in an evil way. Careers have been destroyed, relationships ruined and some people have no idea what it means to have a sense of worth or self-esteem just because someone spoke maliciously against them. No wonder James says: 'Everyone should be quick to listen, slow to speak and slow to become angry,' (James 1:19). James follows up this admonition with one that is even stronger when he says, 'If anyone considers himself religious and yet does not keep a tight rein on his tongue, he deceives himself and his religion is worthless.' (James 1:26.)

Reuben, the oldest and the one who most likely would have blocked the plan to sell Joseph, was not present. If we assume that one or two among the brothers did not really agree with the plan in their hearts, the account shows that they failed to make their doubts known to the rest. Often we think that our little number will not make a difference and therefore we just go along with the crowd. We must remember that the lone voice often has great power. Judah spoke and swayed the opinion of all his brothers. So often the virtuous keep silent because they are in the minority. But they don't

Victory *through* DEFEAT

realise that their saying something could actually lead to many others following their lead.

But what would they really gain by selling Joseph to the Ishmaelites? Come to think about it, that plan was also evil. Indeed, as Judah claimed, 'He is our brother, our own flesh and blood.' The one thing they would gain out of their evil scheme was a guilty conscience which would trouble them for as long as they lived. The idea of selling Joseph was not worth it at all, even if he had been sold for a large sum. May the Lord help us always to do that which is right in his eyes.

The act of selling someone into slavery just shows to what extent the human family had fallen. It had to take the life of God himself to redeem man. How inconceivable, then, that men could even think of selling other men! The worth of even the poorest person is so infinite that it cannot be purchased with money, no matter how big the sum may be. The devil tried to buy the Son of God by suggesting, 'All this, I will give you, . . . if you will bow down and worship me' (Matthew 4:9). Jesus refused to be bought because he knew that such an arrangement apart from being outside the will of God was just not possible. No amount could buy his soul. The idea was, anyway, preposterous, that the Creator could worship the world's greatest sinner.

Moreover, the suggestion to sell their brother just shows how worldly these brothers had become. Although we live in this world of sin, Jesus tells us that we are not of this world (John 17:14). Indeed, as the apostle Paul also affirms, our citizenship is in Heaven (Philippians 3:20). What a way to conduct business! From the beginning of the whole matter right to its conclusion, God is out of the picture. No one stops to ask whether what's being done will be according to the Lord's will. We have a right to make this assertion because these are not pagans. Yet how often we are like them. We conceive plans and carry them out without ever stopping to ask, 'Where is God in all this?' As God's children we must seek his will in every situation.

Strangely, the record states, in a rather emotionless way, that Joseph was sold for twenty shekels of silver to the Ishmaelites who took him to Egypt. It does not describe the overwhelming emotions, the cries and pleas of desperation as the young man is carried away to a strange land. It speaks of the event as though it was unimportant, in a cold, matter-of-fact way. Well, if we find ourselves in a similar situation and the event is trivialised, we must remember this record. If God saw that adding the details of emotion was going to be important to the story, he would have inspired Moses, the author of the book of Genesis, to record the whole picture. True, this is a painful and traumatic experience from a human standpoint. But knowing the glorious ending of the story, we could tell Joseph to leap with joy. Imagine what pain we could be spared if we learned to trust in the providence of God.

Victory *through* **DEFEAT**

Chapter 8

Reuben finds Joseph gone!

'When Reuben returned to the cistern and saw that Joseph was not there, he tore his clothes. He went back to his brothers and said, "The boy isn't there! Where can I turn now?" Then they got Joseph's robe, slaughtered a goat and dipped the robe in the blood. They took the ornamented robe back to their father and said, "We found this. Examine it to see whether it is your son's robe." He recognised it and said, "It is my son's robe! Some ferocious animal has devoured him. Joseph has surely been torn to pieces." Then Jacob tore his clothes, put on sackcloth and mourned for his son many days. All his sons and daughters came to comfort him, but he refused to be comforted. "No," he said, "in mourning will I go down to the grave to my son." So his father wept for him.' (Genesis 37:29-35.)

Reuben's influence, as he was the oldest among the brothers, would have been strong enough to keep Joseph from the misfortune that befell him, if from the beginning he had made his position clear. Reuben did not share his brothers' intention to kill or even sell Joseph. But he was not resolute. He was unstable as water. How like Reuben we are! Inwardly we may be convinced that something is wrong, but we don't have the courage of our convictions.

We must remember that there are moments in life when there are no second chances. When it is within our power to make a

8   *Reuben finds Joseph gone!*

difference to someone or indeed in some matter, we must rise quickly to the occasion. Reuben's grand moment of opportunity was lost. Opportunities to make real differences in the lives of others scream at us from every corner. At home we have an opportunity as parents to speak words that will encourage a discouraged child who is ready to throw in the towel in the fight against sin.

The evil leading to the disappearance of Joseph happened so fast that we can hardly believe that it occurred. His brothers must now begin to face the results of their action. What will they say to their father? Sin always leads its victims to the wall. The brothers have no way back. They must therefore create a tissue of lies. An innocent animal must be sacrificed. Yes, an innocent goat must be slaughtered. Sin is always terrible because it does not just affect those who choose to live by its dictates but many innocent ones suffer as well. Two people – a man and a woman – decide to engage in adultery that leads to an unwanted pregnancy. They are pushed to the wall. The result: abortion.

But the death of an innocent animal illustrates vividly the penalty for sin. Someone must take the blame in order to let the guilty go free. This is exactly what happened when Adam and Eve chose to disobey God. Christ, the innocent Lamb, had to die in order to let sinners go free.

For a while, there is great rejoicing in the camp of the wicked. But God knows the end from the beginning. God knows that it is not over until it is over.

For the survivors death is agonisingly painful. Painful in that it cancels all hope this side of eternity. The one who is struck by the fatal arrow of death is taken for good – removed from loved ones never more to be seen until the resurrection morning. Jacob must face the grim reality of death, the reported death of his son Joseph. Death in this particular instance is doubly painful because it is unexpected. Joseph has been a robust young man, full of energy and life. Suddenly he is gone! To add salt to the painful injury, this is his

Victory *through* DEFEAT

father's boy – the one he loves more than all the others. One would have thought that Jacob, being a holy patriarch, a staunch believer in God, would have taken this moment courageously. After all, he knows about the future resurrection of the righteous. But no, he weeps and refuses to be comforted.

The description of the mourning that is given here gives the impression of the mourning that is characteristic of people who don't believe in God. Writing to the Thessalonians, Paul says: 'Brothers, we do not want you to be ignorant about those who fall asleep, or to grieve like the rest of men, who have no hope.' (1 Thessalonians 4:13.) Jacob was so devastated at the supposed death of his son Joseph that he refused to be comforted. Paul doesn't say we mustn't grieve; rather, he says we mustn't grieve like the rest of men who have no hope. It is OK to cry. As a matter of fact, crying is the natural way to deal with loss. But there is a certain way of mourning that is destructive. This is the kind that Paul is talking about. Here one mourns as though there is no glorious future at the end of the long dark tunnel. This kind of mourning disconnects us from God. It fails to see beyond the misery and trauma of today. It does not see a rainbow in the cloud.

God in his incomprehensible love will use this dark experience to help Jacob recognise a flaw in his life he may not have been aware of. Could it be that Jacob loved the gift (Joseph) more than he loved the Giver?

But the story reveals something also: Men are, after all, men, born from dust. In spite of the many good things that could be said about Jacob, he wasn't perfect. He had areas where he needed to grow. Fortunately, Jacob is not man's example; Christ is. Jacob's story is a story about growth. As long as we are alive and in God there is always room for growth.

8　　　*Reuben finds Joseph gone!*

That God does not come to the rescue of Jacob in his hour of sorrow, by revealing exactly what happened, shows that he works in ways we do not understand. When Herod wanted to kill Baby Jesus an angel 'appeared to Joseph in a dream. "Get up," he said, "take the child and his mother and escape to Egypt. Stay there until I tell you, for Herod is going to search for the child to kill him." ' (Matthew 2:13.) The Magi were also warned in a dream not to go back to Herod. Thus we see the hand of God active in preserving the life of the infant Christ. In our story God does not use any of the more than a thousand methods he has at his disposal to reveal to Jacob what has happened. He lets Satan's game of destruction go on. God's way of looking at things is not man's way. The truth is simply that God has a better view of things than we have. God can see things we can't see. God knows exactly what will be the end of this matter. Life at times may appear to be painful, but one day all will agree that God has done all things well.

As I look at Jacob's deceitful children, I cannot avoid making a comment about their hypocrisy. They are responsible for Jacob's sorrow and now want to act as comforters. With crocodile tears, they stand as Job's comforters. They sold Joseph and did they expect their father simply to trivialise the loss? But we see ourselves in these men. We, too, often act just like that.

But this long dark shadow did not just affect their father but the brothers as well; in fact, everyone at home. When they sold him, they thought they were putting an end to Joseph's dream stories. They thought they would be happy. But their consciences as well as their father's mourning disturbed them. At the time the devil is tempting us, he tries as much as possible to play down the consequences. He dwells so much on the supposed good. However, once we succumb, he quickly shifts his emphasis and makes us realise how terrible the sin we have committed is. For the brothers there was another burden they would continue to carry for many years, the knowledge that Joseph wasn't dead but had simply been

Victory *through* **DEFEAT**

sold. That burden of guilt would haunt them even after Jacob's death.

Yet even at that stage it wasn't too late to confess to their father what they had done. They would have at least saved him the anguish of the knowledge that his son was dead. And maybe even some of their burden of guilt would have been rolled away. But such is the deceitfulness of sin that the sinner would rather live with a guilty conscience than confess. Confession clears away the burden of guilt. True, the consequences may follow, but at least the guilt is taken away. With our confession and repentance, God gives us the opportunity to begin life anew.

While Joseph was crying over his misfortune and while his father was mourning his son's 'death', God was working his purpose out. He was guiding Joseph in a mysterious way.

9

Chapter 9

Joseph arrives in Egypt

'Now Joseph had been taken down to Egypt. Potiphar, an Egyptian who was one of Pharaoh's officials, the captain of the guard, bought him from the Ishmaelites who had taken him there.' (Genesis 39:1.)

My dad used to tell us stories of relatives who had simply 'disappeared' and left no trace. His uncle Mr Jam Mwelwa went to Burma to fight as a soldier in the Second World War. It is assumed that he died there. No one but God knows the exact location and the circumstances under which he died. My great-grandfather, Jim Songesonge, after divorcing his wife (having fathered some children with her), left for Congo and settled there. Most likely he married again and had other children that we know nothing about.

In the passage under consideration, the curtain was closed on the life of Joseph as far as his family was concerned. Yet to God, Joseph's life was just as open as it had always been. Here, through a revelation given to Moses, God is telling the details of Joseph's life. Our enemies may think that they have got rid of us by whatever means, but God keeps our memory very much alive. In this story, as we shall see later, the focus shifts from the brothers to Joseph. Obeying God is the only thing that ultimately brings success.

It is worth noting that while the brothers knew only that Joseph had been sold to the Midianite traders who were going to Egypt, God knew where he finally landed, the person who bought him and what position he held. Isn't it wonderful to know that God knows who we are, where we are, what we do and every detail of our lives? I guess after a while that Joseph's memory among his brothers began to grow dim. But Joseph was as alive as he had always been in the sight of God. And that's ultimately what really matters.

Victory *through* DEFEAT

Potiphar and the entire nation of Egypt have an opportunity to know the living God through what the devil thought would be an end to Joseph's dreams. At the local level, Joseph's life would be a magnet just as it would later be at the national. Potiphar and Egypt are mentioned here only because of their connection with Joseph. We would not have heard of Potiphar had it not been for Joseph. The power of light is indeed significant. Many who lie low, the unimportant and marginalised, would get a new lease of life were they to be in contact with those whom God calls the 'light of the world.' My position as a child of God is what makes it possible for me to write this material and share it with my readers. But even if I were to be a 'star' in the world, without God my influence would simply be negative.

Joseph was sold twice: first by his brothers and then by the Midianite traders. In the eyes of many he appeared just like any ordinary commodity to be traded as people willed. Yet even though he had descended so low, he was still Heaven's prized treasure. God was keeping a close watch over him. What's important, therefore, is not the worth or estimation or price tag that people put on us, but our value in God's eyes. We must remember that Christ was sold for thirty pieces of silver, yet he was the beloved of God. God had this to say about him: 'This is my Son, whom I love; with him I am well pleased.' (Matthew 3:17.) We are valuable in God's eyes whether we are white, black, yellow, men, women, young, old, rich, poor, educated or uneducated.

Chapter 10

Joseph at Potiphar's court

'The Lord was with Joseph and he prospered, and he lived in the house of his Egyptian master. When his master saw that the Lord was with him and that the Lord gave him success in everything he did, Joseph found favour in his eyes and became his attendant. Potiphar put him in charge of his household, and he entrusted to his care everything he owned. From the time he put him in charge of his household and all that he owned, the Lord blessed the household of the Egyptian because of Joseph. The blessing of the Lord was on everything Potiphar had, both in the house and in the field. So he left in Joseph's care everything he had; with Joseph in charge, he did not concern himself with anything except the food he ate.' (Genesis 39:2-6.)

True prosperity can be found only in the Lord. 'The Lord was with Joseph and he prospered'. Joseph put the past behind him and seized the moment that was before him to his master's advantage. Our past can either be negative through our own scheming or through life's inevitable twists that we have no control over. We must pick a day – TODAY. Today is a day for renewal in the strength of God. It doesn't matter what past experiences we have had.

Joseph had heard great stories of the great God from his father Jacob. Now he wished that God of his father to be his as well. It was not enough simply to speak about 'the Creator, Sustainer God who helped my father in his time of distress.' Joseph must now claim his own share of that Creator, Sustainer God. Because of that important choice, 'The Lord was with Joseph.' And because the Lord was with him, Joseph prospered.

Interestingly Joseph prospered while living 'in the house of his

Victory *through* DEFEAT

Egyptian master'. Joseph found himself at Potiphar's house because he was sold there. While his circumstances were far from being ideal, God blessed and made him prosperous just where he was. Joseph made the most of his surroundings, fitting God into his programme. The result was a blessing right where he was. Is God a part of the programme I am in? The house might be small, circumstances not ideal, but is God a part of what I am doing and where I am? I am sure Joseph was often tempted to think of the good home-life he had suddenly lost. But he came to terms with his present reality and sought the guidance of God on how best to deal with his new situation. The encouraging thing is that God is able to work with any situation. Circumstances don't have to be good in order for God to be God and for him to grant us success.

Without doubt, Joseph was a diligent worker. He worked hard, while he trusted in the Lord. Whatever his hand found to do, he did it with all his heart. After all that's what the Scriptures bid us do: 'Whatever you do, work at it with all your heart, as working for the Lord, not for men,' (Colossians 3:23). There was no magic there. God did not grant success to indolent and slothful workers. Joseph demonstrated in a practical way what it means to work as a child of God. Is it not shameful that often as God's people we do not follow Joseph's example? We must remember that Joseph was not a church worker. He was not even a prophet or priest. He was in secular employment all his life, yet he exemplified what it meant to live and work as a child of God. Indeed, God's people are supposed to give of their best in the things they do.

Joseph gives a powerful demonstration of the kind of witnessing we ought to give wherever we find ourselves: 'His master saw that the Lord was with him and that the Lord gave him success in everything he did. . . .' Potiphar recognised something extraordinary about Joseph. Undoubtedly, Joseph talked often about his God, but more than that his life demonstrated that connection. The results of his relationship with God were conspicuous to his master. God was visible to Potiphar because of who Joseph was. It was not just a private relationship. Potiphar saw that the Lord was with Joseph. In a relationship that is like the one we are talking about here, others must be able to give a testimony of seeing God's working in and through us. His blessings to us must be conspicuous to others, not just to ourselves. So it was that from a mere houseboy Joseph became a steward, the highest position in the home. We are reminded that it is God's intention to make his faithful people heads and not tails (see Deuteronomy 28:13). The position of a head is, however, earned; it does not come on a silver platter.

The position of a steward is beautifully highlighted. The things belonged to Potiphar, not to Joseph. Joseph was simply the head steward. In that position he performed so well that 'the Lord blessed the household of the Egyptian because of Joseph. The blessing of the Lord was on everything Potiphar had, both in the house and in the field.' How do I fare as the Lord's steward? Do I add value to my Master's estate? Have my Master's things become more valuable, more appreciable as a result of my handiwork? Our passage further states: 'so he [Potiphar] left in Joseph's care anything he had.' Can my Master trust me in this way? Can he trust me with the work allotted to me?

Through Joseph, 'the Lord blessed the household of the Egyptian.' Can it be said that through me, my children, family, friends and relatives have received a blessing? For as salt and light we are called to touch lives, to leave a trail of blessing where we pass. We are called to speak words that will comfort, bless and heal. Can it indeed be said about us and about our church that through us it has pleased God to bless the community around us?

The Bible says that Joseph was successful in 'everything he did'. What a beautiful way to live – having success in everything one does! God is not merely interested in granting us success in one or two things or several. God wants to grant us success in all things. The key, though, is to be where God wants us to be and to be found doing what he wants us to do.

Chapter 11

Joseph is tempted by Potiphar's wife

'Now Joseph was well-built and handsome, and after a while his master's wife took notice of Joseph and said, "Come to bed with me!" But he refused. "With me in charge," he told her, "my master does not concern himself with anything in the house; everything he owns he has entrusted to my care. No one is greater in this house than I am. My master has withheld nothing from me except you, because you are his wife. How then could I do such a wicked thing and sin against God?" And though she spoke to Joseph day after day, he refused to go to bed with her or even to be with her.' (Genesis 39:6-10.)

In Joseph's life, there was nothing the devil could use to bring him down. What a life! Joseph was a perfect example of what every child of God should be. True, God loves us the way we are. He accepts us the way he finds us at any given point. But he loves us too much to leave us the way he finds us. It is no secret that God would love his children to be like him, to be distinct from the world, to be transformed into the likeness of his Son Jesus Christ.

Finding nothing in Joseph's life to discredit him, Satan took advantage of Joseph's well-built and handsome body. A gift intended to show in a limited way God's workmanship was seized by Satan to harm Joseph. How many have fallen when lured by this subtle satanic temptation! Pampered, praised and idolised for some special gift given them by God, they have left the narrow path for the broad way. That which people praise us for may become a means of our own falling when God is out of the picture.

This passage shows also that we don't just struggle with self and other internal challenges. There is a world out there bent to destroy

Victory *through* DEFEAT

us. In the world, if you are infatuated with love so falsely called, you should get whom you want and sleep with them. That's the view. The world is out to get Joseph, out to strangle him. Temptation in the story came from the master's wife. On the surface this woman had everything, yet she was empty. Life outside of God is simply no life at all; it is an illusion, a shadow. It is simply an experiment, not an experience. There is always an insatiable passion to try this and that in the hope of finding happiness. Unfortunately (or is it fortunately?), happiness outside of God is always outside of our grasp.

Joseph was tempted and indeed there is often little or nothing we can do about temptation that comes our way. We might not be in a position to prevent temptation from coming, but we are always in a position to make a choice in the matter. As the saying goes, we cannot prevent birds from flying above our heads but we can prevent them from making nests in our hair. Joseph chose to say 'No' to temptation.

His reasons for saying 'No' are two-fold. From them we derive principles to live by. Firstly, Joseph argues from the principle of natural justice. How can he do such a thing against a master who has been so kind and good to him? On that one count, Joseph says he can't do what the master's wife is asking. This reasoning is important, especially in view of the fact that Joseph is addressing a woman whose life is not hid in God. Even though she doesn't probably believe in the God of Heaven, the reason Joseph gives is good enough to make sense to her.

As God's people we must consider the consequences of our actions, not just to ourselves but to those we love. 'If I break this commandment, what are the consequences to my spouse, children, friends, church members and the society at large?' Our lives do not

Joseph is tempted by Potiphar's wife

just belong to us to be used or abused as we feel. We have a host of other significant people out there who 'own' us and are going to be broken and affected by our wrong course of action.

But then Joseph goes on to ask the all-important question: 'How can I do such a wicked thing and sin against God?' Joseph in effect is saying, 'Even if my other submission doesn't make sense to you, my refusal to sleep with you still stands, because it would be sinful in the eyes of God to do such a thing.' Some issues indeed will not make sense to some people no matter how much we try to explain things. In the end, therefore, what matters is our allegiance to God. This is the great principle to live by.

The passage says that the woman continued her sweet talk in spite of Joseph's persistent refusals. Satan, we must remember, does not give up easily. He will use everything at his disposal to make sure that we succumb. He will nag and pester to wear out our patience. And more importantly he will do everything he can to dilute the intensity of our conviction on the matter.

Victory *through* DEFEAT

Chapter 12

Joseph is sent to prison

'One day he went into the house to attend to his duties, and none of the household servants was inside. She caught him by his cloak and said, "Come to bed with me!" But he left his cloak in her hand and ran out of the house. When she saw that he had left his cloak in her hand and had run out of the house, she called her household servants. "Look," she said to them, "this Hebrew has been brought to us to make sport of us! He came in here to sleep with me, but I screamed. When he heard me scream for help, he left his cloak beside me and ran out of the house." She kept his cloak beside her until his master came home. Then she told him this story: "That Hebrew slave you brought us came to me to make sport of me. But as soon as I screamed for help, he left his cloak beside me and ran out of the house." When his master heard the story his wife told him, saying, "This is how your slave treated me," he burned with anger. Joseph's master took him and put him in prison, the place where the king's prisoners were confined.' (Genesis 39:11-20.)

This is not the case of an idle mind being the devil's workshop. Temptation to Joseph came right when he was busy doing his work with all the integrity and devotion he could muster. Joseph woke up one morning to find himself in a situation he was unable to escape. Please, someone, explain what had happened to all the help this

Joseph is sent to prison

young man of integrity should have received. Where was God? Wherever God was, why did he allow his trusted and faithful child to be trapped in that way? How could the one who trusted in God so much be abandoned to perish so shamefully? For the second time when it really matters, God is suddenly nowhere in the picture – so it seems. The one who trusted in God is, suddenly, abandoned in the midst of nowhere. What do we make of this?

Joseph's tenure as an attendant in Potiphar's house comes to a sudden and shameful close. It is time to move to another appointment and God alone knows where. What a way to make a transition, yet God allows it. At this point we cannot even speculate why things have happened this way. There seems to be no explanation. We must wonder why God would elect to graduate his son from this learning experience to another in such an unorthodox way. If Joseph has completed his course in Potiphar's house, why not allow a better scenario to prevail, as he moves to the next assignment?

From the outset it should be mentioned that God was witness to what was going on. But if God was witness to what happened, why did he allow things to happen that way?

Joseph had been wronged by his father's partiality and indulgence. Faults had been encouraged that were now to be corrected. He was becoming self-sufficient and exacting. God witnessed everything and knew exactly how to respond.

God will allow Satan to employ his evil principles in his warfare against his children. Joseph was falsely accused. This is one way in which Satan discourages God's people. In the case in point, the idea is two-fold: to discredit Joseph and to chill his spirit and ultimately make him lose his hold on and confidence in this God who does not seemingly save him from trouble. But strangely God uses this same method to make Joseph even stronger. It is strange but true that trials make pure gold. God's people don't become strong by being protected from trials and adversity but by having to confront them. They must work in the minefield of trials in order for them to grow

Victory *through* DEFEAT

into the likeness of their Maker. Jesus put it well when he said: 'If anyone would come after me, he must deny himself and take up his cross and follow me', (Matthew 16:24). The cross has always been a symbol of suffering, adversity and trial, and – ultimately – death itself.

Contrary to Satan's intentions and expectations, Joseph was made stronger as a result of the fiery temptations he kept conquering. 'Consider it pure joy, my brothers, whenever you face trials of many kinds, because you know that the testing of your faith develops perseverance. Perseverance must finish its work so that you may be mature and complete, not lacking anything.' (James 1:2-4.) Further, James says, 'Blessed is the man who perseveres under trial, because when he has stood the test, he will receive the crown of life that God has promised to those who love him.' (1:12.) Jesus, speaking on a similar subject, says, 'Blessed are you when people insult you, persecute you and falsely say all kinds of evil against you because of me. Rejoice and be glad, because great is your reward in heaven, for in the same way they persecuted the prophets who were before you.' (Matthew 5:11-12.)

Truly, for Christianity to make sense, it must be clothed in Christ's robe of righteousness. One has to be born again in order to be a genuine Christian. How else indeed can one rejoice in the midst of persecution? How does it make sense to 'consider it pure joy, my brothers, whenever you face trials of many kinds?' Dr Elden Gerald Kamwendo had just moved from Solusi University where he had been working as the academic dean to assume the position of education director at the Adventist Church's headquarters in the Southern Africa Indian Ocean Division, Harare. He looked bright, healthy and ready to face the challenges of his new work when I talked with him the day I met him at the office in December 2005.

12 *Joseph is sent to prison*

One day in mid-April he was flying from the USA to Harare via Johannesburg, South Africa. Upon arrival at Harare Airport, he collapsed and was rushed to the Avenues Clinic where he died a few days later. When I heard the news of his death, I thought of his wife and children and the difficult and traumatic months or even years that lay ahead of them. For Mrs Kamwendo and the children, that was undoubtedly a severe trial. How would they make sense of James's inspired statement that says, 'Consider it pure joy, my brothers, whenever you face trials of many kinds'? Certainly, when I stood by the entrance of the University Teaching Hospital in Lusaka and heard the heartbreaking news that my dear wife Martha and brother Alex had passed away in a tragic car accident, I did not consider it pure joy.

I repeat: the only form in which Christianity makes sense is the New Birth. Any other form will simply bring disappointment, disillusionment, stress, frustration and discouragement. We thus owe it to ourselves as Christians to heed the words of our Lord Jesus when he says, '. . . no one can enter the kingdom of God unless he is born of water and the Spirit.' (John 3:5.) To appreciate Christianity we must be born again. James says that 'the testing of your faith develops perseverance.' Perseverance is a necessary quality if Heaven is our goal.

Jesus says, 'Rejoice and be glad, because great is your reward in heaven.' Apart from the internal staying power that trials bring, they have a beautiful reward at the end of time: eternal life. 'He who stands firm to the end,' Jesus said, 'will be saved.' (Matthew 24:13.)

But what about the strange silence of God at critical times? While I cannot answer for Joseph, I do know that God has come out very loudly and clearly on the issue of trials in his Word. Let's consider a few texts now.

'Let us run with perseverance the race marked out for us. Let us fix our eyes on Jesus, the author and perfecter of our faith, who for the joy set before him endured the cross,' (Hebrews 12:1-2).

Victory *through* DEFEAT

'Fear not, for I have redeemed you; I have summoned you by name; you are mine. When you pass through the waters, I will be with you; and when you pass through the rivers, they will not sweep over you. When you walk through the fire, you will not be burned; the flames will not set you ablaze.' (Isaiah 43:1-2. See also 2 Corinthians 6:4-10; 11:23-28; and Romans 8:28, 35-39.)

When going through what we deem to be undeserved trials, we like to ask, 'Why me?' Maybe even Joseph was tempted to ask it, especially in view of the fact that he was a faithful young man. Why Joseph and not some other young man? Only God can answer that question. We cannot speculate. In the book of Isaiah there is a useful passage that helps us understand the mystery of trials: 'Woe to him who quarrels with his Maker, to him who is but a potsherd among the potsherds on the ground. Does the clay say to the potter, "What are you making?" ' (Isaiah 45:9.) God knows what he is doing with his children. The One who made us knows exactly what to do in order to make us into honourable vessels. Trials are some of the means by which God fits or shapes us into his image.

Even though he is a God of love, oftentimes we shall not understand why he allows certain things to happen the way they do. God will often appear to be contradictory. Habakkuk says: 'Your eyes are too pure to look on evil; you cannot tolerate wrong. Why then do you tolerate the treacherous? Why are you silent while the wicked swallow up those more righteous than themselves?' (Habakkuk 1:13.) Interestingly, Habakkuk would later conclude: 'Though the fig-tree does not bud and there are no grapes on the vines, though the olive crop fails and the fields produce no food, though there are no sheep in the pen and no cattle in the stalls, yet I will rejoice in the Lord, I will be joyful in God my Saviour.' (Habakkuk 3:17-18.)

We may try to construct our religion on the evidence of sight, but

the structure will collapse. The Bible says that 'the righteous will live by his faith' (Habakkuk 2:4). Paul says, 'We live by faith, not by sight.' (2 Corinthians 5:7.) Faith is defined in the Bible as 'being sure of what we hope for and certain of what we do not see.' (Hebrews 11:1.)

Joseph could have chosen to co-operate with Potiphar's wife. But the 'easy' option is not necessarily the right one in the sight of God. The easy way out would have made him continue to work for Potiphar and avoid prison, but God would have been out of the picture. The presence of God in our lives and in the things we do is the greatest blessing we can ever have in this life. We must be prepared to guard that at whatever cost.

The Bible tells us that Joseph ran away after Potiphar's wife grabbed him and insisted that he slept with her. There are times when the only right thing to do is to run away from a difficult situation.

Here we must stray a bit and talk about Potiphar's wife. God gives us opportunities to become like him – following Jesus' example. Potiphar's wife was given a chance to witness the grace and beauty of a life hid in God in the life of Joseph. The idea was not simply for her and the entire household to marvel at grace but to produce a desire in them to follow Joseph's leading. Unfortunately, as things turned out, she was immune to the Spirit's pleading. She didn't need to live that way. But I must turn to myself and ask how things are going with me. God continues to bring opportunity after opportunity through the different situations that come my way. His own Word brings out opportunities for change. Do I just marvel at those opportunities or do they move me into a path of change?

Potiphar's wife knew that she was telling lies. It didn't matter how convincing her case appeared to be. The entire household might have believed what she said but that didn't change the truth; she was lying. It doesn't matter how many people may believe me to be genuine. It doesn't even matter if I have forced myself to believe my

Victory *through* **DEFEAT**

own lies. I could pose as a genuine Christian when in truth I am not. I may be accorded respect by those who think I am sincere, yet I know in my innermost self that I am simply living a lie.

What we do in secret may appear simply to end there – in secret, but let's always remember that there's Someone who sees what's happening.

It's interesting that the Bible is silent about Joseph's reaction to this false accusation. Nothing is mentioned about what he says, if indeed he says anything. There is no voice from Heaven to reveal the truth. In the case of Mary and Joseph, for example, when Joseph discovers that his wife-to-be, Mary, is pregnant, he decides to pull out secretly, being a godly man himself and not wanting to subject Mary to public disgrace. In this particular scenario an angel of the Lord appears to him in a dream and reassures him that what he is assuming is not what has happened. But in the case of the young Joseph, God simply leaves matters as they have been fabricated.

There are times when silence is golden. God is silent and so is Joseph. With the kind of 'evidence' that's available, unless God himself comes in, it is impossible for Joseph to defend himself. May God grant us wisdom to know when to speak and when to keep quiet.

It is likely that Potiphar knew that his wife was lying. If he had believed the accusation, Joseph would have been executed.

The prize for being faithful to God? In this case, a prison sentence. Joseph goes to prison while John the Baptist has his head cut off. Jesus observed: 'Whoever finds his life will lose it, and whoever loses his life for my sake will find it.' (Matthew 10:39.)

Chapter 13

Joseph excels
in prison

'But while Joseph was there in the prison, the Lord was with him;
he showed him kindness and granted him favour in the eyes of the
prison warder. So the warder put Joseph in charge of all those held
in the prison, and he was made responsible for all that was done
there. The warder paid no attention to anything under Joseph's care,
because the Lord was with Joseph and gave him success in
whatever he did.' (Genesis 39:20-23.)

Paul states in Romans 8:35: 'Who shall separate us from the love
of Christ? Shall trouble or hardship or persecution or famine or
nakedness or danger or sword?' He goes on to answer his own
question: 'No, in all these things we are more than conquerors
through him who loved us.' (Romans 8:37.) He goes on: 'For I am
convinced that neither death nor life, neither angels nor demons,
neither the present nor the future, nor any powers, neither height
nor depth, nor anything else in all creation, will be able to separate
us from the love of God that is in Christ Jesus our Lord.' (Romans
8:38-39.) There is simply no method the devil can use to snatch us
out of the hand of God. True, we may choose to defect, but God loves
us so much that no single scheme of Satan can succeed in getting us
out of the gripping hand of God. God's personal presence of love is
promised to every believer. 'While Joseph was there in the prison,
the Lord was with him.' Well did the psalmist put it: 'Even though I
walk through the valley of the shadow of death, I will fear no evil, for
you are with me;' (Psalms 23:4). What a powerful blessing is God's
personal presence in our lives! I can wallow in poverty and even be
burned at the stake if God is with me. With God's presence I can
face any situation. As Paul put it: 'I can do everything through him

Victory *through* DEFEAT

who gives me strength.' (Philippians 4:13.)

The Lord was with Joseph. We must remember though that Joseph had no monopoly over the blessings of the Lord. To each child of God is promised sonship and the attendant blessings. The question that each of us must ask himself after reading this is simply: 'Is the Lord with me?' For we must not be content in knowing only what God did for Abraham or Joseph but also what he has done for us; what he is doing for us.

God showed Joseph kindness. Kindness is an attribute of love. 'Love is kind.' (1 Corinthians 13:4). Kindness is a self-giving attribute of love. Kindness which always flows out of love gives out something that benefits the recipient. Consider, for example, the prayer of Abraham's servant: 'O LORD, God of my master Abraham, give me success today, and show kindness to my master Abraham. See, I am standing beside this spring, and the daughters of the townspeople are coming out to draw water. May it be that when I say to a girl, "Please let down your jar that I may have a drink," and she says, "Drink, and I'll water your camels too" – let her be the one you have chosen for your servant Isaac. By this I will know that you have shown kindness to my master.' (Genesis 24:12-14.)

God showed Joseph kindness by granting him favour in the eyes of the prison warder. The warder put Joseph in charge of all the prisoners and he was made responsible for all that was done there. The godly manner in which Joseph conducted himself made him stand out above every other prisoner. It should be noted that while God's people can and are to be found in all walks and spheres of life, they must be different from others by their behaviour.

For Joseph, religion was always a public and not just a private matter. It stood out in stark beauty and attracted the attention of the highest officer in the prison. May it be said of all children of God that

13 *Joseph excels in prison*

they are of such a godly disposition that they attract the attention of those with whom they come into contact. God's people must first and foremost stand out because of their deeds of love.

Interestingly, Joseph was in his number one slot, showing that it had nothing to do with his circumstances or place. The life of God in us has to shine through in spite of where we may be and what we are doing. God's child doesn't have to have a ministerial position in order to do his work well. With Joseph at the helm you could be sure that prisoners benefited from his God-given administrative skills. As a child of God, Joseph dispensed his duties with integrity, fairness, efficiency and effectiveness.

Thus while Joseph was young he saw the reality of God's presence in his life both in bad and good times. God is indeed real when we let him be the controller of our lives. He is a present help in times of need.

Victory *through* **DEFEAT**

Chapter 14

Joseph is released from prison

"Then the chief cupbearer said to Pharaoh, "Today I am reminded of my shortcomings. Pharaoh was once angry with his servants, and he imprisoned me and the chief baker in the house of the captain of the guard. Each of us had a dream the same night, and each dream had a meaning of its own. Now a young Hebrew was there with us, a servant of the captain of the guard. We told him our dreams, and he interpreted them for us, giving each man the interpretation of his dream. And things turned out exactly as he interpreted them to us: I was restored to my position, and the other man was hanged.' (Genesis 41:9-13.) To get the full details read chapter 41 of Genesis.

The occasion that brings the name of Joseph to the forefront is the troubling and disturbing dream Pharaoh has had. God's answer to Joseph's plight comes in the most unusual way. One morning he wakes up to be told that he is needed at the royal court.

God decides to create a situation. He sends two disturbing dreams to Pharaoh that none of the wise men and magicians can interpret. It is this failure to interpret the dream by the so-called wise men that leads the cup-bearer to remember the young Hebrew prisoner he met while serving a short prison sentence at the house of the captain of the guard. Joseph is immediately summoned to the king's palace.

Standing before the highest man in the land, Joseph is told why he is there: 'I had a dream,' says Pharaoh, 'and no one can interpret it. But I

have heard it said of you that when you hear a dream you can interpret it.' (Gen. 41:15.) Joseph is quick to correct the notion that he is capable of doing that, for he knows that the whole thing is the work of God. He says: 'I cannot do it, but God will give Pharaoh the answer he desires.' (Gen. 41:16.) Joseph has learnt the beautiful lesson that 'Every good and perfect gift is from above' (James 1:17). Joseph knows that he is simply a channel. He himself cannot do what Pharaoh is asking of him. But he knows that 'nothing is impossible with God.' (Luke 1:37.)

Two things come out of Joseph's response that need to be mentioned. Firstly, for Joseph to be so confident that 'God will give Pharaoh the answer he desires', there must be something about his relationship with God. Joseph is not an average believer. Even though Joseph is an Old Testament character, he knows what it means to live with Christ in heavenly realms. His mind is soaked with the realities of Heaven. He knows what it means to 'Set your minds on things above, not on earthly things.' (Colossians 3:2.) Joseph had a heart to heart and mind to mind relationship with his Maker. He thus was able to know that what Pharaoh was asking was something within the will of God. The Holy Spirit revealed to him that there was work to be done where he stood, as the matter had been determined by God himself.

So many times we come across situations where our help is desperately needed, but we don't know how to relate because we are not in touch with the One with whom nothing is impossible. Even when we think we know the mind of God, we are not able to help because we lack the necessary power. We are empty wells. And as someone has said, it is not possible to draw water out of an empty well.

But where does Joseph get the confidence that even though God has the power to do the impossible he will do it in this particular situation? Let's face it. Many of us Christians have been in situations where we were absolutely convinced that God was going to perform a miracle but he did not. One Christian lady lost her husband in sudden and unexplained circumstances. As he lay on the bed pronounced dead, she was asked to rush over to the clinic so she could take a look at the body

Victory *through* DEFEAT

before it was taken to the mortuary. Upon arrival, in utter shock and disbelief, she remembered that her situation was not an impossible one. She still had one more thing she could do. The body did not need to be taken to the mortuary. Here was an opportunity to demonstrate the power of God. Summoning every spiritual muscle she could muster, she prayed that Jesus would raise her husband back to life. Unfortunately, the husband did not revive. She was to cry time and again as she remembered that disappointing episode. She could not understand why God did not perform a miracle when it was within his power to do so.

So how can Joseph be so sure that God will grant this request? Is he not putting his own life at risk? Where does he get the courage and confidence to trust God in such a way? Joseph had put God to the test in the most ordinary situations of his life. He had asked God to help him in his work and in his relationships with other people. He had proved that God was real in his personal life in daily trials and labours. His was not a God who could be summoned only at the eleventh hour when he needed rescue. The problem with most of us is that God becomes necessary only when our lives or those of family members are at stake. We don't take God seriously in our daily living. God is taken seriously only when we or someone dear to us is about to drown. It is then that we look for him, for then we are sure he is the only one with life-saving skills.

Twice Joseph has suffered keen disappointment. First, when he was forcibly carried off from the land of the Hebrews. Like all of us, Joseph would have gladly welcomed a miracle from God. God did not save him from that traumatic experience. He let his brothers sell him to the Ishmaelites, those Midianite merchants travelling to Egypt. He had done nothing to deserve such a harsh deal. Then came the imprisonment he suffered for refusing to do something evil in the sight of God. Joseph could have felt angry with God for 'letting him down.' But he bore his trials with patience and dignity. Though he did not understand why things had to happen that way, he continued to trust in the God of mercy and love who reigns on high. He could say with Habakkuk: 'Though the fig-tree does not bud and there are no grapes on the vines, though the olive crop fails and the fields produce no food, though there are no sheep in the pen and no cattle in the stalls, yet I will rejoice in the Lord, I will be joyful in God my Saviour.' (Habakkuk 3:17-18.) It is not so much at the eleventh hour when we need God as in the daily routines and relationships. After all, eleventh-hour moments come only once in a while, and, when they do, they often come as crises.

I remember once telling my children Mwape and Mwila something which, I hope, made sense to them. I had just moved to Lusaka from Harare where I had been working for almost ten years. My kids had come home on holiday from their high school at Maxwell in Nairobi. A day later they told me that they wanted to move to their friends' house 'where there's fun, for this place is boring.' It was more than a year since I had lost my wife in a road traffic accident. I was therefore relieved that the kids had come so we could spend two weeks together. They did not want to live with me because a number of things they would have liked to play with were still held at the warehouse at Stuttaford. I had decided not to get the luggage from Stuttaford because in a couple of months I was going to be returning to Zimbabwe to teach at Solusi University. Naturally, the place was boring for them. And, of course, it was true that as youngsters it was natural that they would want to be with their friends. Not wanting them to feel guilty but at the same time making sure the point was driven home, I said: 'You know, guys, I feel good when you are around. You have been gone for quite a good while now and I am just so happy that we can spend these two weeks together again. But sometimes you give me the impression that all you care to receive from me is things. Just imagine how I will feel at the end of two weeks when you come back from your friends and it is time to go, and you want me to provide your school requirements. I feel as though you just want to use me.'

Victory *through* DEFEAT

They, of course, protested and said it was not like that. 'No, Dad, it's just that it's so dull and so boring here. We won't take two weeks,' Mwila said. But sometimes I get this feeling that God often feels we are just interested in him when we want things from him. We do not have a love relationship whereby we miss him not so much because of the physical benefits we get from him but because he is a loving Friend to be around with and, of course, he is our everything.

The bottom line is that God knew Joseph intimately. Through God's revelation, Joseph was able to see heavenly realities that many of us are strangers to. God's intentions for us are glorious ones. He wants to do wonderful things for us that are beyond description. God wants to give us 'the Spirit of wisdom and revelation, so that you may know him better.' (Ephesians 1:17.) He desires that 'the eyes of your heart may be enlightened in order that you may know the hope to which he has called you, the riches of his glorious inheritance in the saints, and his incomparably great power for us who believe.' (Ephesians 1:18-19.)

Note that Egypt for a time becomes the focal point of God's glorious intentions, not because of Pharaoh and all his people but because of one God-fearing young man named Joseph. Joseph lives in a dungeon and is known only by a few people in Egypt. Television networks, radio reporters and the dailies of the day, if indeed they had been there, would never have wasted their time on covering a story that would not be of public interest. Yet the One who created all things will step in to make known the story of Joseph that will reach beyond the borders of Egypt and indeed beyond the borders of time. What an honour! Two thousand years ago, people had the opportunity to read the inspiring story of Joseph. Today, we, too, have the chance to read one of the most beautiful and powerful stories in Scripture. 'Those who honour me,' God says, 'I will honour,' (1 Samuel 2:30). And one beautiful thing about this narrative is that it prompts the reader to desire to emulate the life of

14   *Joseph is released from prison*

Joseph. Many received coverage in Scripture as a result of the wicked things they did. But what awful revelations!

Interpreting the dream was important because it would help Pharaoh understand the meaning. However, that was not sufficient. There was a need to know what to do and who was to do it. God granted to Joseph the wisdom to interpret the dream and to craft the plan that would meet the challenges that lay ahead. 'Because there will be plenty,' Joseph said, 'it is important that a fifth of the harvest be kept as a reserve for the hard and severe times ahead.' It should be a matter of concern to God's people that often it is secular people out there who come up with innovations that help mankind solve the world's problems. What has happened to God's people? Is it not a shame that matters should be like this? God's people are supposed to be creative and innovative. God is the author of creativity. If we share in his nature then we ought to be seeing more and more of God's people being at the forefront in providing solutions to the many ills of our world. I am impressed to hear Pharaoh confess: 'Since God has made all this known to you, there is no one so discerning and wise as you. You shall be in charge of my palace, and all my people are to submit to your orders.' (Genesis 41:39-40.)

The fact that God provided through Joseph the meaning of the dream as well as the way to tackle the problem that arose shows how comprehensively God deals with situations. Of what benefit would it really have been if the only thing that was made known was the meaning of the dream? 'A challenge will come your way as a nation,' God says. 'There will be plenty of food in the next seven years, but remember not to be like the New Testament rich fool who harvests plenty, puts it in barns and begins to eat from that. You can begin to eat from your reserves only when the seven years of famine are upon you.' Paul, writing under the Spirit's inspiration, would later say: 'No temptation has seized you except what is common to man. And God is faithful; he will not let you be tempted beyond what you can bear. But when you are tempted, he will also provide a way out so that you can stand up under it.' (1 Corinthians 10:13.)

Victory *through* DEFEAT

Pharaoh is the highest man in the land. But Pharaoh is not connected to the true source of power. In the eyes of the One who knows what really counts this is a serious flaw. We all like power because it is sweet, but unless power is used according to God's will, it can prove deadly. Without God, man continues to grope in darkness. Joseph, on the other hand, walked with God even though he was in prison. The kind of power Joseph had is what God is interested in our having, because that's real power.

Pharaoh asks an interesting question about Joseph: 'Can we find anyone like this man, one in whom is the spirit of God?' (Genesis 41:38.) This is interesting because this is Joseph's first time to meet Pharaoh. Yet in this brief encounter Pharaoh can see something unique in Joseph. A child of God does not need a week to prove that he is one. The demeanour, the speech and the little things will have a telling effect upon the people we come into contact with. Oh, how I pray that I can exhibit that heavenly conduct that would allow me to be seen as a child of God! I do not want to be mistaken for a child of God because I preach a good sermon but because I live one. Joseph was not a pastor in the technical sense, yet he was so vibrant in his relationship with God that through and through he radiated the power of God in his life. Statements like 'God was with Joseph' colour the landscape of his life. Joseph's inner life was as transparent as his outward life.

'Can we find anyone like this man, one in whom is the spirit of God?' That's the question the world must be asking today. All too often the world has been cheated by those of us who claim to know God. God presents a very crystal-clear picture of himself and his principles in his Word. Anyone who sees that picture will also see the beautiful colours of love that are painted on every page of scripture. But do we, who claim to know God, really radiate that love? Can the world believe in God by what they see in us? Scepticism, cynicism and the lack of interest in

14

Joseph is released from prison

the things of God may have much to do with the fact that the world has not found 'anyone like this man, one in whom is the spirit of God.' May the reader pause here and ask himself the penetrating question: 'Does the Holy Spirit dwell in me?' Let's be honest, for we lose nothing by admitting our problems. Are we truly born of the Spirit, born from above? Do our children, spouses, friends, workmates and acquaintances see the kind of spirit Pharaoh saw in Joseph? Let's not fool ourselves. Our title with all the respect it brings, our education, our profession, our status in society and whatever else we may think of as our hiding place will not help us if our inner life is flawed. Jesus said: 'What good will it be for a man if he gains the whole world, yet forfeits his soul? Or what can a man give in exchange for his soul?' (Matthew 16:26.) Here nothing will help but brutal honesty. We are dealing with a life issue that's like nothing else in terms of importance. I must ask myself the million-dollar question, 'Am I born again?' Has George Mwansa truly died to give way to Christ? Is George Mwansa dying on a daily basis to allow Christ to be the visible one in his life? Listen to Paul as he makes his case on this important matter:

'But whatever was to my profit I now consider loss for the sake of Christ. What is more, I consider everything a loss compared to the surpassing greatness of knowing Christ Jesus my Lord, for whose sake I have lost all things. I consider them rubbish, that I may gain Christ and be found in him, not having a righteousness of my own that comes from the law, but that which is through faith in Christ – the righteousness that comes from God and is by faith. I want to know Christ and the power of his resurrection and the fellowship of sharing in his sufferings, becoming like him in his death, and so, somehow, to attain to the resurrection from the dead.' (Philippians 3:7-11.)

Feel the pulsating passion as Paul further states in Galatians 2:20: 'I have been crucified with Christ and I no longer live, but Christ lives in me.'

I used to know a sister who was quite close to me. She died because she hid her problem for too long. Every so often you would hear her

Victory *through* **DEFEAT**

complain about pain in the stomach. But that was just an indication of a bigger problem she had. She had contracted a deadly sexually transmitted disease. She found it hard to disclose the fact to those who could have helped. The problem became bigger and the pain more intense, but she kept telling the people that it was abdominal pain. Consequently, she was given medication intended to treat pain in the abdomen – medication to treat a symptom and not the real problem.

When it finally got to the point where she could not hide her problem any longer, it was, unfortunately, too late. The disease had reached a stage where it was impossible, humanly speaking, to cure. She died a painful death that could have been avoided had she been honest with others. Someone reading this could be struggling with a sin that he is simply unwilling to confess before God. No matter how palatable, and therefore difficult for you to forsake, that sin may be, God is able to root it out of your life if you give it up to him. He is able and willing to forgive and to cleanse for 'If we confess our sins, he is faithful and just and will forgive us our sins and purify us from all unrighteousness.' (1 John 1:9.) God could not have put it more strongly when he said: 'Come now, let us reason together, . . . Though your sins are like scarlet, they shall be as white as snow; though they are red as crimson, they shall be like wool.' (Isaiah 1:18.)

'Then Pharaoh said to Joseph, "Since God has made all this known to you, there is no one so discerning and wise as you. You shall be in charge of my palace, and all my people are to submit to your orders.' (Genesis 41:39, 40.) Firstly, notice that Pharaoh has taken the point very well. In all that he has said, Joseph does not rob God of the praise due to him. He does not give himself a portion of credit and assign the rest to God. Look at all these statements that Joseph emphasises in his speech to Pharaoh: 'God has revealed to Pharaoh what he is about to do', 'God has shown Pharaoh what he is about to do', 'The matter has been firmly

14 *Joseph is released from prison*

decided by God, and God will do it soon.' Even when it comes to offering advice, Joseph does not offer himself to be the one to execute the huge task at hand. He says, 'And now let Pharaoh look for a discerning and wise man and put him in charge of the land of Egypt.' (Genesis 41:33.) Pharaoh is convinced that this young man has simply been God's channel, a conduit if you like. We must never seek self-gratification just because God provides us with an opportunity to represent him in a special way. However proficient we may become at doing something for God, we must always remember to give glory and credit back to the Giver. Pharaoh will go away from this encounter with a knowledge of truth that saves. It is not about Joseph and his special abilities; rather, it is about the God of Heaven who makes known his will to his servant.

'You shall be in charge of my palace and all my people are to submit to your orders,' Pharaoh says to Joseph. The young man can hardly believe what he hears. 'I, a prisoner, suddenly to become the second most important man in this foreign land? Am I hearing right? Is this a dream?' Potiphar, under whose custody Joseph was held, would have been around at that important meeting. But even if he was not, news must have very quickly filtered to him that Joseph had been elevated to the second highest position in the land. His wife, the woman who had fabricated the story that led to Joseph's imprisonment, also heard quickly what had happened. Knowing the truth as she did, Potiphar's wife must have felt that that kind of vindication could come only from God, the God of Joseph. In the twinkling of an eye things had changed. The prisoner was now in a position to command with incredible authority and power.

Even Satan cannot believe what he is witnessing. Satan had first incited Potiphar's wife to tempt Joseph, but that plan had failed. Furious that he couldn't get the young man to sin, he used a false accusation to get Joseph into prison. By doing that, Satan had hoped to silence the young man. God is a genius. Time and again Satan has tried the method of silencing God's people in this way, but results have often proven disastrous for him. The very method he uses to grind God's people in the dust becomes the method God uses to elevate them.

Victory *through* **DEFEAT**

Well, they sent Joseph to prison to teach him a lesson; now prison has become a stepping-stone for Joseph. His own brothers who sold him in the first place had no idea that far from teaching him a lesson they were simply promoting him.

Potiphar's wife must have been scared out of her wits. She is dreading what Joseph will do now that his power is even greater than that of her husband. Surely the first thing Joseph must do is to 'sort out' all those who were responsible for sending him to prison. Madam Potiphar knew that Joseph was innocent and justice must therefore take its course.

But Joseph was a solid man of God. Had he decided to seek retribution, the Scripture would have told us so. Vengeance belongs to the Lord. And in any case the experience of passing through prison is what ultimately made it possible for Joseph to climb to that number two position in the land. Joseph would therefore not waste time using a hammer to kill a fly. He had more important issues to think about and to deal with.

To be a man or woman of God means doing things the way God would do them. Hanging on the cross for the sins that were not his, Jesus said: 'Father, forgive them, for they do not know what they are doing.' (Luke 23:34.) If the Spirit of God dwells in us we shall be compelled by the love of God to offer forgiveness to others, remembering that we, too, have been shown mercy.

While attending a church meeting in St Louis, Missouri, I watched a video that showed the spirit of forgiveness at work. A Tutsi young man had killed the husband of a certain Hutu lady during the genocide that took place in Rwanda in 1994. Later, tables were turned. The young man was arrested and put in prison. The lady whose husband was killed visited that young man and gave him a Bible as a present and started praying for him. Later when he was released from prison, he was taken by the same woman whose husband he had killed. He was staying at her house at the time the video was shown. I must be quick to add here that for this kind of thing to happen one has to be born again.

The reward that Joseph receives tells me something about God that is often not thought of when times are hard. Joseph might even have been tempted to think that God had abandoned him to a life in a dungeon. He could have harboured the thought that God did not reward right doing. Let's face it: in moments of discouragement these kinds of thoughts bombard our minds more often than we care to admit. God always rewards faithfulness. It may take a long time but the reward will surely come. Joseph had been faithful in Potiphar's household. And he had been faithful in prison. I think of the words of our Lord Jesus in his parable of the talents when he said to each one who had made use of his talents: 'Well done, good and faithful servant! You have been faithful with a few things; I will put you in charge of many things.' (Matthew 25:21.)

The change is dramatic. One who had become used to wearing rags as a prisoner is now dressed in fine clothes. His chains of servitude are exchanged for a chain of gold. From prison to palace! After thirteen years of servitude, Joseph is handsomely rewarded.

We also see how all of creation can serve the purposes of God. A heathen king who doesn't even know him becomes an instrument in blessing a child of God. Who would have thought that Pharaoh would acknowledge the King of whom he had only heard? While he could be thinking that he was responsible for bestowing honour upon Joseph, we believe that Joseph himself knew better. It came from God above who can use any situation or person to supply the needs of his children. He used ravens to feed Elijah at one point and a poor widow to take care of him at another. (See 1 Kings 17:1-16.) God is ever mindful of his children, but it takes a Christian of Paul's stature to say: 'I have learned to be content whatever the circumstances. I know what it is to be in need, and I know what it is to have plenty. I have learned the secret of being content in any and every situation, whether well fed or hungry, whether living in plenty or in want. I can do everything through him who gives

Victory *through* **DEFEAT**

me strength.' (Philippians 4:11-13.)

Just as the Lord needed many years later to counteract the influence of the Egyptian court on the life of Moses before he became a suitable candidate for leadership, so with Joseph, a young man wronged by his father's partiality and indulgence, the Lord knew exactly how to teach humility so that through him great things could be accomplished.

15

Chapter 15

Joseph marries

'Pharaoh gave Joseph the name Zaphenath-Paneah and gave him Asenath daughter of Potiphera, priest of On, to be his wife.' (Genesis 41:45.)

The marriage of Joseph is an interesting one. He had at that time reached the age of thirty. Pharaoh heaped tokens of his esteem on him. Inspiration tells us that Pharaoh gave Joseph 'Asenath, daughter of Potiphera, priest of On, to be his wife.' Priests wielded a strong influence on Egyptian worship. Socially, the marriage enhanced Joseph's standing among the Egyptians. However, Asenath was a heathen. Joseph must have remembered the story he heard from his father about how his great-grandfather Abraham had sent his servant to his country and his own relatives to get a wife for his son Isaac. (Genesis 24:4.) Isaac was Joseph's grandfather.

Abraham as a worshipper of the true God did not want his own son, heir to the promise, to marry a woman from among the Canaanites because they were heathens. Joseph could have also remembered another story told him by his father. The story says that 'When Esau [Joseph's uncle] was forty years old, he married Judith daughter of Beeri the Hittite, and also Basemath daughter of Elon the Hittite. They were a source of grief to Isaac and Rebekah.' (Genesis 26:34.) Apart from getting into a polygamous situation, Joseph's uncle Esau married unbelieving women. The story continues: 'Then Rebekah [Jacob's mother and Joseph's grandmother] said to Isaac, "I'm disgusted with living because of these Hittite women. If Jacob takes a wife from among the women of this land, from Hittite women like these, my life will not be worth living." ' (Genesis 27:46.)

Victory *through* DEFEAT

Isaac her husband must have been influenced by his wife's comment. He 'called for Jacob [Joseph's father] and blessed him and commanded him: "Do not marry a Canaanite woman. Go at once to Paddan Aram, to the house of your mother's father Bethuel. Take a wife for yourself there, from among the daughters of Laban, your mother's brother." ' (Genesis 28:1-2.)

Joseph undoubtedly must have thought about those stories depicting the importance of not marrying women who were not of his ancestors' faith. But, nevertheless, he took the woman whom Pharaoh gave him and married her, and apparently had a successful marriage. What then do we make of statements from Scripture that repeatedly warn against marrying women not belonging to our faith?

Firstly, we need to look at this marriage in the light of its context which is rewarding Joseph for his interpretation of Pharaoh's dream and his subsequent counsel regarding it, thereby preserving the lives of the king and all the Egyptians during the seven years of hunger that were ahead.

Secondly, we must remember Joseph's own complicated past. For thirteen years he had been a slave, incapable of going back to his homeland. A slave had very little freedom. Joseph had been bought and became the property of his owners. He had become assimilated, as it were, into his new home country.

Thirdly, during Joseph's employment at court, a wife given in this manner would reveal the working of providence in the life of Joseph. Joseph's acquiring of a wife was not an arbitrary choice but a gesture of love from Pharaoh, acting as it were under the influence of God himself.

Chapter 16

The seven years of abundance

'And Joseph went out from Pharaoh's presence and travelled throughout Egypt. During the seven years of abundance the land produced plentifully. Joseph collected all the food produced in those seven years of abundance in Egypt and stored it in the cities. In each city he put the food grown in the fields surrounding it. Joseph stored up huge quantities of corn, like the sand of the sea; it was so much that he stopped keeping records because it was beyond measure.' (Genesis 41:46-49.)

We must commend Joseph, Pharaoh and all the Egyptians for heeding the counsel of God. This dream was prophetic. Pharaoh and his people could have chosen to ignore it at their peril. The Bible is full of end-time prophecies for end-time people. In Matthew 24 Jesus gives a discourse on the signs of the end of the age. Every child of God would do well to read both Matthew 24 and 25 often. 'Now learn this lesson from the fig-tree: As soon as its twigs get tender and its leaves come out, you know that summer is near. Even so, when you see all these things, you know that it is near, right at the door.' (Matthew 24:32-33.) These signs of the end of the world were not given to satisfy our curiosity but to help us get ready for the coming of the Master. Joseph went throughout Egypt during the seven years to collect the food. He was faithful to the message that God had given him. The Egyptians were told that there would be plenty of food in the next seven years. I am sure that many decided to take advantage of the coming bumper harvest to grow more than they had ever grown before.

Just imagine what would happen if we spread the message of the coming Lord seriously. Clearly, the world would be lighted with the glory of the Lord and Jesus would come. Joseph in this sense gives an example of what God's end-time people ought to be doing. God's people must be busy everywhere, proclaiming the message of the soon-returning King. We have the authority to do this from God himself. He asks his people today to take this message to every nation in order that everyone might have an opportunity to hear it and to make a decision. Sad to say that for many of us our love for God has grown cold 'because of the increase of wickedness' (Matthew 24:12). We have 'a form of godliness but denying its power' (2 Timothy 3:5).

Just as the Lord had said, during the seven years of abundance, the land produced plentifully. However, it was the action of collecting food and storing it in the cities that brought meaning to the dream. God has determined that one of these days the world, as we know it, will come to an end, whether I am ready or not. Someone has said that to be forewarned is to be forearmed. The world will end to usher in eternity's abundance for the righteous ones.

We must mention something here about our physical existence. Jesus said: 'Man does not live on bread alone . . .' (Matthew 4:4). Physical food while not as important as spiritual food is nevertheless necessary. Food is a factor in fighting diseases, giving us strength and making us grow. God gave us food for that purpose. The idea of storing up a portion of what was produced in the seven years of abundance is a timeless principle. Life is unpredictable. We must learn to save for the rainy day. To do that is not to deny our faith. I am imagining what could happen in the undeveloped countries of the world if something as simple as storing food in reserve for each city, town and village were done. If centres in each district would be established to oversee the implementation of this mechanism, what would happen to national food security? Properly utilised, the kind of

The seven years of abundance

plan we see established by God in Egypt would benefit many nations of the world. If this cannot be done at a national level for whatever reasons, one can still use this principle of saving for the rainy day.

We see the obvious fact that food is critical to the survival of nations. Governments must learn to invest heavily in agriculture. Where it is possible, agriculture should be the mainstay of each nation's economy. Agriculture, generally speaking, has a way of involving the least capable man in the nation, as everyone can at least grow something. Mining, oil exploration and things like these usually benefit only huge multilateral corporations. The common people rarely benefit.

For many years my own country, Zambia, invested heavily in the copper-mining industry and paid only lip service to agriculture. Zambia was at one time one of the leading producers of copper in the world. Beautiful towns were built in the copper-mining belt. There was money for free education from the first grade to university, and money for free medical services. But one day we woke up to be told by those who control the economic systems of the world to sell our mines to private firms. The government at that time had been the major shareholder in the mines. This economic arrangement, it was argued, had led to the mismanagement and eventual collapse of that national asset.

The selling of the mines and many other parastatal companies was dubbed privatisation. Being the inhabitants of a poor country, we did what we were told and the mines were sold for a pittance. Unfortunately, at a time when the mines were doing extremely well, the government had not developed a sustainable and viable agricultural system. We still depended on rain for watering the crops. With all the money the country was making through the sale of copper, leaders should have thought of developing a mechanised agricultural system. Zambia is blessed with rivers and lakes that will never dry. Arable land is also plentiful. But the leadership did not think of giving agriculture the place it deserved. As I write this book, Zambia is one of the poor nations of the world, because agriculture is not a developed mechanised industry. The majority of the farmers are of peasant stock and rely only on hoes and ox-drawn ploughs to cultivate land. Of course there are other factors like corruption and mismanagement of resources, but the non-development of a viable, mechanised agricultural programme is a major contributor to national poverty.

Chapter 17
Joseph the father

'Before the years of famine came, two sons were born to Joseph by Asenath daughter of Potiphera, priest of On. Joseph named his firstborn Manasseh and said, "It is because God has made me forget all my trouble and all my father's household." The second son he named Ephraim and said, "It is because God has made me fruitful in the land of my suffering." ' (Genesis 41:50-52.)

Joseph's firstborn son, Manasseh, is named that way because God has made Joseph, the father, 'forget all my trouble and all my father's household.' Notice again the prominent role God plays in Joseph's life. Joseph is now Governor of Egypt. It is not that he doesn't remember where he came from and the circumstances that led him to Egypt, but these things no longer bother him. He has healed. The pain is gone. But what's important is that he recognises that God is responsible for the healing. God has used a series of events to bring it about. The good news here is that it doesn't matter what type of pain we may have to go through; God will finally bring us healing if we place ourselves, as Joseph did, in his hands. In the case of Joseph it took more than thirteen years to bring that healing about. God treats each case differently. I lost my wife and my young brother in a tragic road accident. A couple of days earlier I had lost my sister through an illness. Needless to say, it was a very painful and traumatic experience. As I write this book one year later, the pain of that loss is not as intense as it used to be. I have not lost the memory of what happened, but God has been slowly but surely taking away the poison of pain and trauma.

Manasseh will always be a reminder of God's goodness in turning around the life of Joseph. Joseph had lost his family, and had been sold into slavery. Yet he had emerged victorious from that fiery

Victory through DEFEAT

furnace. He could look back and see how God had used each of those events simply as stepping-stones to a life he could never have dreamt of. The ashes of his sorrow and shame had been turned into joy and gladness.

In his second born, Ephraim, Joseph saw another miracle of God: 'God has made me fruitful in the land of my suffering.' When Joseph arrived in Egypt he had nothing. Now, on top of all the material blessings he has received from God, he can boast of the blessing of children. Joseph's name will not die with him. Children are a heritage from the Lord. Only God is capable of bringing life into existence. Thus Joseph is right when he says, 'God has made me fruitful in the land of my suffering.'

Only God can grant a fruitful existence in this world – this land of suffering. Very often our suffering will dim our eye of faith. God will be seen as a distant, abstract force with little interest in the affairs of some of us. We would do well to remind ourselves about a letter God asked Jeremiah to write to the Hebrews who had been taken as captives into Babylon by King Nebuchadnezzar. Part of the contents of that letter said: 'This is what the LORD Almighty, the God of Israel, says to all those I carried into exile from Jerusalem to Babylon: . . . "For I know the plans I have for you," declares the LORD, "plans to prosper you and not to harm you, plans to give you hope and a future." ' (Jeremiah 29:4, 11.) The captives are assured that they have a life beyond captivity. In fact, not just beyond captivity but while they are still in captivity. God says to them:

' "Build houses and settle down; plant gardens and eat what they produce. Marry and have sons and daughters; find wives for your sons and give your daughters in marriage, so that they too may have sons and daughters. Increase in number there; do not decrease. Also, seek the peace and prosperity of the city to which I have carried you into exile. Pray to the LORD for it, because if it prospers, you too will prosper." ' (Jeremiah 29:5-7.)

The Bible speaks of God's people as 'aliens and strangers on earth' (Hebrews 11:13). A key concept among these pilgrims is suffering. Suffering has always been a hallmark of God's people. The New Testament book of Hebrews 11:35-38 describes it this way:

'Others were tortured and refused to be released, so that they might gain a better resurrection. Some faced jeers and flogging, while still others were chained and put in prison. They were stoned; they were sawn in two: they were put to death by the sword. They went about in sheepskins and goat-skins, destitute, persecuted and ill-treated – the world was not worthy of them. They wandered in deserts and mountains, and in caves and holes in the ground.'

Yet in the midst of their suffering God makes them fruitful in many ways. Though they are persecuted and killed they are not wiped out. Their numbers keep on increasing from age to age, for without them God would destroy the earth. In the midst of their suffering, God gives them authority to take the message of salvation to all the nations of the world: 'Therefore go and make disciples of all nations, baptising them in the name of the Father and of the Son and of the Holy Spirit, and teaching them to obey everything I have commanded you.' (Matthew 28:19-20.) It is both a miracle and paradox that those who must endure suffering, persecution and even death would at the same time experience numerical and spiritual growth. This for me is a powerful indication that God is at work in the world. In this sinful world of suffering, God will continue to make his children fruitful. He has promised to be with them till the end of the age. (See Matthew 28:20.)

Victory *through* **DEFEAT**

Chapter 18
The seven years of famine

'The seven years of abundance in Egypt came to an end, and the seven years of famine began, just as Joseph had said. There was famine in all the other lands, but in the whole land of Egypt there was food.' (Genesis 41:53, 54.)

As had been predicted, when the seven years of plenty came to an end, the seven years of famine began. The interesting thing about this period is that all the countries came to Egypt to buy grain from Joseph. In this harsh story of a physical famine can be learned important spiritual truths. In fact, for the Bible reader the point is really not about the historicity of this event but what spiritual lessons can be learned from it.

As human beings we have a tendency to take the blessings of God for granted. We could be enjoying health, wonderful social relationships, good marriages and often not even care to guard these blessings jealously. It is only at the point when we are diagnosed with a life-threatening disease that we care to listen to the principles of good health. God's plan was for the Egyptians to take advantage of the good seven years of plenty and make reserves for the rainy day. Under Joseph's wise leadership, they did just that.

God's plan for each one of us is to use what he has given us

wisely, for we don't know what tomorrow may bring. God expects us to maximise our opportunities and potential today as a preparation for tomorrow. Each day must become a building block for tomorrow. When the famine came, the Egyptians were ready for it while the other nations, who were ignorant of what was coming and therefore couldn't prepare, began to languish. The prophecy which God had given in a dream to Pharaoh began to yield its positive results.

God instructed Noah to warn the people about a flood that would destroy the world. God would 'put to an end to all people, for the earth is filled with violence' (Genesis 6:13). Noah was instructed to build an ark which all who would believe could enter and thus be saved. As Noah built, he also preached a message of warning. Although the people heard him preach, they didn't take the message seriously. The flood came and except for Noah and his family, who believed, all the people were destroyed by the flood.

Jesus concluded his sermon on the mountain by saying, 'Therefore everyone who *hears these words of mine and puts them into practice* [emphasis mine] is like a wise man who built his house on the rock. The rain came down, the streams rose, and the winds blew and beat against that house; yet it did not fall, because it had its foundation on the rock.' (Matthew 7:24, 25.) And James goes on to remind us: 'Remember, it is a message to obey, not just to listen to. If you don't obey you are only fooling yourself. For if you listen and don't obey, it is like looking at your face in a mirror, but doing nothing to improve your appearance.' (James 1:22, 23, author's paraphrase.)

Notice that Joseph was responsible for selling food to the Egyptians and those who came from other nations. This physical famine reminds us of the great spiritual famine ravaging the world today. Everywhere one goes one finds a general decline in the spiritual life of people. Christianity, the once vibrant movement

Victory *through* DEFEAT

of the apostolic period, has become so emptied of its power that the majority of its adherents show only its form rather than content. To compound the situation, there are millions of people around the world who don't even know that there is such a thing as the Good News that tells of a loving Saviour who came to die in order to redeem mankind. The famine is severe. May the Lord revive his people, the remnant people, to whom he revealed a long time ago what would become of this world.

Oh that I may be a Joseph to whom the world will come to buy the grain of salvation! We must, as God's people, humble ourselves, pray and seek his face so that he may heal us. There is a world out there that's dying in sin, a world ravaged by the severe famine of the Word of God. Hungry people scattered everywhere across the world don't know where to go and buy the grain of salvation. Oh Lord God, Mighty One of Israel, revive your Church once again. Dear reader, I ask you to pause here to join me so we can pray for a revival of true godliness. Will you take the challenge to be transformed into the likeness of Jesus so that you may be enabled to understand the moment in which you live today? God is looking for men and women like Joseph to distribute the grain of salvation to a dying world.

Joseph provides a beautiful example of what Christ meant when he said, 'You are the salt of the earth.' (Matthew 5:13.) Salt, apart from giving taste and seasoning to food, has preservative properties. When I was a young boy we once lived in Nchelenge, a small town in Zambia by Lake Mweru. Many people who live around that area are fishermen. My dad used to work for what was then the department of fisheries. The lake was just a stone's throw from where we lived. We often went to the shore to watch the activities of fishermen. There was fish

they used to call *salele* because it was preserved by putting a great deal of salt and drying it in the sun. I used to wonder why they put so much salt until I asked. I was told it was to preserve the fish from getting rotten.

Jesus used the imagery of salt to show us that he expected us to be agents of 'preservation' in this world. Through one righteous man, Egypt and the surrounding nations were preserved from extinction. As salt of this Earth, we are expected to be God's agents of 'seasoning' and 'preservation' in our neighbourhoods, at our workplaces, and everywhere we are found. It must be remembered that the end result of all this seasoning is that those who don't know God might know him and consequently be drafted into his Kingdom.

Victory *through* **DEFEAT**

Chapter 19

Joseph's brothers go to Egypt

'Then ten of Joseph's brothers went down to buy corn from Egypt . . . for the famine was in the land of Canaan also.' (Genesis 42:3-5.) To appreciate this chapter the reader is advised to read Genesis chapter 42.

As we have just read, the severe famine that swept across Egypt was felt in Canaan as well. It is natural to think that God would have spared his people who were living in Canaan. After all, they were his children. Fortunately, it is in this same story of Joseph where we discovered that God did not save Joseph from being sold by his brothers to the Midianites. And even when he chose to be true to God rather than sin, Joseph was not saved from going to prison. To belong to God as his child does not save one from painful situations. After all, they may be the very means God may want to use to save us. It sounds paradoxical but is nevertheless true. Pain, far from being destructive, may enlarge our vision in dimensions we may never have dreamt of.

Ten of Joseph's brothers went down to buy grain from Egypt. Undoubtedly, that country held bad memories for them for it was to Egypt that they had sent their own brother. If I could be allowed to use a bit of sanctified imagination here, I see them discussing Joseph. It's been over twenty years since they sold him, but the

terrible scene appears as though it happened yesterday. The devil is quick to suggest evil. He will push it with all the force he can muster. If that doesn't work, he will try to sweet-talk us into sin. He will leave no stone unturned. But once we have sinned, he abandons us to the consequences of the wrongdoing he had in the first place initiated. 'How could you even think of doing that?' he will say and hang around to taunt us and burden us with guilt.

Joseph's brothers can't stop wondering whatever became of their brother. Egypt is a bad place to visit, for it reminds them of their terrible sin and of their lies to their father about what had happened. No matter how hard they try to suppress the fact, it comes now and then to haunt them. Peace has eluded them these past more than twenty years. Egypt would be the last place on earth they would want to travel to. They are here only because of the severe famine that has affected their area.

Bowing before Joseph, the governor of Egypt responsible for selling grain, the ten brothers have no idea that this is the one they had sold into slavery. Joseph's brothers had fixed a negative stamp on his life. They had hoped to confine him to a life of perpetual misery. Had Joseph allowed anger, frustration and bitterness to drive him, he would indeed have been miserable. But Joseph quickly learned to depend on God. He did not allow his brothers but God to define who he was going to be. Even though it could be said that physically speaking he lived in Egypt, Joseph knew that his real citizenship was in Heaven. Paul reminds us of this in his letter to the Philippians (Philippians 3:20). Indeed, as God's people we have been raised up with Christ and seated together with him in the heavenly realms (see Ephesians 2:6). In God our lives are determined in a certain way. Once this truth is learnt and internalised, it doesn't matter what situation we may find ourselves in; our status remains that of children of God.

Joseph's encounter with his brothers in these changed circumstances reminds me of a story I heard about a man who was

Victory *through* DEFEAT

abandoned by his father when he was born. His mother died while he was young and his uncle took him in and looked after him. It is said that when he was a boy there was nothing about him that indicated that he would grow up into a man of worth and honour. He struggled socially and even academically. But one day he became the president of his nation. His father who had abandoned him then tried to claim him as his own. The once-despised boy refused to acknowledge that he was this man's son.

I always look at young boys and girls with reverence, no matter whether they are from the streets or the palace, because only God knows what they will become one day. The other day I met a street kid who asked me for money so he could buy some food. I asked him what he was doing in the streets when his friends were busy learning at school. He told me that he was living with his grandmother who was too poor to help him with school fees. 'Do you know that one day you could become president of this country?' I asked him. 'If God wills, yes,' he responded. Then I told him the story of a young boy who was once a street boy but later became president. 'You, too, could become president of Zambia, but you must go back to school.' 'I would like to go back if somebody could buy me some books and a pen and pencil.' I took out some money and told him to buy the supplies he was looking for and wished him God's blessings. God alone knows what will become of that boy.

I am also reminded of my own situation as I was growing up. Way back in primary school between the grades of five and seven, I specialised in noise-making. It was practically impossible for me to attend a class without at some point making a noise or poking fun at someone. I remember my grade seven teacher at one school getting so mad with me and suspending me from attending class until I could bring my parents. My dad was a serious no-nonsense man. I couldn't see how I could ask him to come to school for problems I had simply created for myself. I therefore just went to school but never got to enter the class. For almost a week it went on like that until the teacher pitied me and took me back in again.

That behaviour continued in high school. In my first form (grade 8) at St Clement's Secondary School in Mansa, I soon developed a reputation for being noisy and disruptive. One day Mr Doepker, a Canadian who used to teach us mathematics, got so angry with me that he grabbed me by the collar, shouting, 'I can kill you, boy!' as he pushed and led me to the administration block to see the headmaster. There was a distance of about 250 metres between our classroom block and the administration building. He kept holding me so tightly by the collar as he dragged me that I almost choked. Outside by the dining hall some senior students basking in the sun saw the drama and could not but wonder what I had done. Needless to say, I was severely punished, though that did not stop me from being a nuisance.

At the same school while in form two I got into serious trouble. One evening as I was going to class, I saw an Indian teacher by the name of Mr Monteiro passing. He was driving a small turtle-shaped VW car. I shouted at him a name I heard senior students call him: 'Mfumbwa.' I didn't know what it meant. Mr Monteiro heard me and stopped his car. He rushed at me and grabbed me by the arm and led me to the staff lounge. I smelled disaster. Once we got inside the lounge he pounced on me like a lion and turned me into a punching bag. 'Why did you call me Mfumbwa?' he asked in annoyance. 'Do you know the meaning of that word?' Since I didn't know, I just kept quiet as he continued to unleash blow after blow on me. That incident, however, did not help in the least in stopping me from being troublesome.

When I left to study for the ministry at Solusi University I was still badly behaved. All the four years I spent at Solusi studying to become a pastor were spent in noise making. I made noise in class,

Victory *through* **DEFEAT**

in the dormitory and in the library. I was not a serious student. It was only when I went for graduate studies at Andrews University that I became sober. At that time I was married and had been in the work for more than five years. A girl who knew me while at Solusi one day met me on the campus of Andrews University and asked what I was studying. I said theology. She was surprised. 'How come you are studying something you never studied at Solusi?' she asked. 'I was studying theology even at Solusi,' I said. She was surprised. She had thought I was studying business there.

But today I am so thankful that God has changed me into a civilised human being. He is not through with me yet. I still have a long way to go but I am glad to say that I am on the right path. No one who knew me in primary and high schools would have ever thought that one day I would become a child of God, a minister in the house of the Lord for that matter. Only God knows what each one of us is capable of becoming through his grace.

The ten brothers' situation here also shows that, no matter how long it takes, unconfessed sin will ultimately show up to condemn us. It may finally fade from our memories and we may not even experience its deadly effects this side of eternity, but a time will come when the sins we have been unwilling to confess will confront and condemn us.

Chapter 20
The grand reunion

'As he looked about and saw his brother Benjamin, his own mother's son, he asked, "Is this your youngest brother, the one you told me about?" And he said, "God be gracious to you, my son." Deeply moved at the sight of his brother, Joseph hurried out and looked for a place to weep.' (Genesis 43:29, 30.) The reader is advised to read chapters 43-46 in order to appreciate fully the message covered in this chapter.

Jacob's ten sons must make another trip to Egypt because of the biting famine in the land. The youngest son Benjamin is also to be taken, for the man who had sold them grain had insisted that they bring him along or else he would consider them to be spies. For us who read this story we know that the man in Egypt is Joseph, and the reason he insists that they bring the youngest brother is that he wants to see him. Joseph knows what's happening here; so do we, the readers. The brothers, who sold him, and their father Jacob are in total darkness.

God in this particular situation and in several others in scripture gives the reader an opportunity to see life's complex twists and turns. Were we to be in the shoes of the brothers, we would have no idea of how God was weaving our lives behind the scene to shape our present and future. Their father Jacob is dreading the potential loss of Benjamin to some fate. He is convinced that Joseph is dead. The confinement of Simeon back in Egypt does not help matters for the aged patriarch. He cannot understand why things are happening this way, especially when he remembers that his own father Isaac had blessed him. If, indeed, that blessing from his father was genuine, why would sorrow accompany him? Could it be that because he had cheated his father in receiving that blessing, God

Victory *through* DEFEAT

had somehow made it null and void? But what about all those promises he had received from God concerning the future, bright promises of a bright future? Why did the present reality seem contrary to what God had promised him?

To the actors in the drama in Canaan, God is a mysterious Being who cannot be understood. We, the readers, can jump ahead and see the conclusion. We know that God is just about to give his children a glorious reunion and future. Their lives are about to be changed in a dramatic fashion.

It is said over and over again that God is good all the time. The truth of this statement, however, is questioned so many times in our lives when things are not going well for us. After the death of his mother, my 12-year-old son, Brainerd Mwila, asked me how God could be said to be love 'when he takes away one's mother?' In the story of Joseph readers are given a glimpse of the hand of God at work in a seemingly confusing situation for Jacob and his ten sons.

Jacob can only hope that Benjamin will not be harmed. The ten brothers can only hope that the ugly and ruthless claws of disaster will not strangle them. As we read on, we see how an apparently beautifully flowing story becomes tragic. The brothers get to Egypt and all seems to go well. Their fears are dispelled when Joseph, the governor, whom they don't recognise as Joseph, even organises a banquet for them. After buying grain they set off the following morning for their home. Up to this point everything is OK. However, unknown to them, their brother Joseph has set a trap for them by instructing the steward who was serving them to put his silver cup in the mouth of the youngest one's sack. Hardly have they moved far from the city when hell breaks loose. Joseph's steward has been instructed: 'Go after those men at once, and when you catch up with them, say to them, "Why have you repaid good with evil? Isn't this

The grand reunion

the cup my master drinks from and also uses for divination? This is a wicked thing you have done." ' (Genesis 44:4-5.) The situation has now turned ugly. Doom and her sister demon gloom are celebrating in front of the Hebrew captives. With knocking knees, trembling hearts and sagging faces they set off back to Joseph's palace. If in the past they have escaped from difficult situations, they know that they cannot escape from this one.

Yet this sad retracing of their footsteps to Joseph's palace will prove to be the grand moment of their lives, which are about to be changed in ways they have never dreamed or imagined. Sadness will turn into joy. Doom and gloom will flee in shame. God is about to prove that he is good all the time. They are about to receive evidence of that.

Back at Joseph's palace the drama continues with the suspense of a Hollywood movie. When Joseph finally reveals his true identity, his brothers are terrified. Joseph could throw them into prison for what they did many years ago. In reassuring language, Joseph says to them: 'I am your brother Joseph, the one you sold into Egypt! And now do not be distressed and do not be angry with yourselves for selling me here, because it was to save lives that God sent me ahead of you.' (Genesis 45:4-5.) What follows is something we could hardly believe if we were unbelievers. This story sounds too good to be true in this world of sin. But it is true. Soon Joseph's brothers are on their way to Canaan to announce the sweetest news their aged father has ever heard: 'Joseph is still alive! In fact, he is ruler of all Egypt.' (Genesis 45:26.) The Bible says that Jacob was stunned and could not believe them. 'But when they told him everything Joseph had said to them, and when he saw the carts Joseph had sent to carry him back, the spirit of their father Jacob revived. And Israel said, "I'm convinced! My son Joseph is still alive. I will go and see him before I die." ' (Genesis 45:27-28.)

And so it was that the aged patriarch Jacob set out for Egypt with all that was his and his children and their children. 'As soon as

Victory *through* **DEFEAT**

Joseph appeared before him, he threw his arms around his father and wept for a long time. Israel said to Joseph, "Now I am ready to die, since I have seen for myself that you are still alive." ' (Genesis 46:29-30.) What a grand reunion!

The Bible tells us in Romans 8:28 that 'we know that in all things God works for the good of those who love him, who have been called according to his purpose.' The story of Joseph is a classic example of this principle at work. What started as a tragic story with nothing good ever seeming to come out of it ends in a glorious, majestic, grand finale. This is indeed a case of victory through defeat. What a God!

George Mwansa is a lecturer in the school of theology and religious studies at Solusi University, Bulawayo, Zimbabwe. He has served in the past as district pastor, conference and union departmental director, lecturer at the Zambia Adventist Seminary, and communication director for the Eastern Africa and Southern Africa-Indian Ocean Divisions. As communication director he also served as editor of *Outlook* (Eastern Africa Division general paper) and *Adventist Echo* (Southern Africa-Indian Ocean Division general paper). He studied at Solusi University before he went for graduate studies at Andrews University.